Rescuing a Dying Organization

Geary Reid

ISBN: 978-976-8305-06-0

Acknowledgements

Great thanks must be expressed to the following people:

The heavenly Father, for granting me the wisdom and inspiration to record the information in this book, which I began on February 10, 2018, and completed on March 3, 2018; my family, for their continued encouragement and support regarding various challenges; and several people who have assisted with reviewing and editing the book:

- Christine Spencer-Coates, BSc. & Dip. in Pub. Mgmt.
- Shellon Garner, ACCA, CAT
- Pastor Jocelyn Dolphin
- John A.S. Clowes, MSc., BSc., Dipl.
- Judah Louisy, MSc, ACCA, FCPA
- Dexter Cox, MBA
- Terrence Thomas, Diploma in Land Surveying

To you, the reader: have fun while reading, and grasp and practice what you learn so that this world will become a better place. Many people are depending on your guidance. We all need a shoulder to lean on and a hand to guide us.

Geary Reid
MBA, FCCA, FAAPM, MPM, CAT

Reid's Learning Institute and Business Consultancy

reidnlearn.com

Amazon: amazon.com/author/gearyreid

Facebook: Reid n Learn

Instagram: Reid n Learn

LinkedIn: Reid's Learning Institute
and Business Consultancy

199 Kuru - Kururu, Soesdyke Linden Highway
Guyana, South America

Contents

Pictorial view of the sections of this book

At Death's Door
Learning from the Past
Fully Recovered

Introduction

A dying organization is not a dead organization! It is a sign indicating that death is near. However, many organizations showing signs of death can be rescued.

Often, medication is needed. In this case, it needs someone who has the skills to implement the rescue operation.

Checking for a pulse is an important initial stage in rescuing an organization. When the organization is about to die, a quick rescue operation is needed, and a mature medical practitioner will look for a pulse first.

Most organizations have vital organs. These organs must be protected so that the organization can stay alive. If the problem is not detected, then the organization can fall into the same situation again and again and then probably die.

This book is divided into three sections, which intends to highlight the stages:

- At Death's Door
- Learning from the Past
- Fully Recovered

Not everyone is able to learn from the past, but those who do can have great gains for the future. Organizations should never be satisfied with failure but should constantly strive for success. Success is not always easy to achieve. It must be carefully planned, and with dedication, the results will be positive.

Many organizations may experience downtimes, but that must not be their permanent state. An organization must never accept failure as a norm but must work toward success. When an organization becomes successful, it may have a positive impact on the entire community and nation as a whole. Organizations must find ways to improve. An organization may not always be able to generate additional revenues, *but monitoring costs is important for its success.*

Making your products and services known to the public should be part of your marketing plan to help your organization stay alive. Some of the gains of an organization must be kept for later days. Savings and investments are important for keeping extra funds and possibly generating some additional revenues.

With a visionary captain, an organization has a higher potential for success than another organization within the same sector. The visionary captain can see a brighter future while others only see failure. The steady head and eyes of a visionary captain will help an organization make a mark in society.

Success is possible for all organizations. Go for success and avoid failure.

Section 1: At Death's Door

Nonprofit organizations are established to provide products or services for the benefit of society, while profit-making organizations are mainly concerned with generating profit for themselves. The greater the profit, the more financial and social gains.

Sometimes, in an attempt to make profit, an organization engages in various activities and experiences several challenges. These challenges may become so problematic that there may be a need for medical attention. Many times when medical attention is sought, the organization is already at death's door. When an organization is at this stage, then a diagnosis is needed. This is a preliminary requirement for many medical officers when someone shows signs of lifelessness or dysfunction.

The medical practitioner has to perform many functions to locate a pulse. These attempts may be time-consuming but cannot take too much time since any delay may lead to death.

Having a matured medical practitioner available may help rescue the organization. However, not all attempts to save a dying organization will result in continued life.

Identifying the main organs (departments) is always critical for the successful rebirth of an organization. When time is against you, you must utilize your time wisely. Your attention must be focused on the main departments. When those departments are identified and attention is placed on them, they can begin to give life to the rest of the organization.

To help a dying organization, the root of the problem must be identified. If the main problems are not identified, then the organization may fall into the same problem again. One good example is an individual who is discharged from the hospital and goes home, but he goes back for the same reason. Therefore, finding the root of the problem and addressing it is the best way to resolve an issue.

The attempt to find the problem may be time-consuming, but if you want to help the organization, you have to find what caused the problem. When the cause is found, then efforts must be made to reduce, eliminate, or remove it from the organization. Solving some problems may be costly, but it may be the only way to address the problem.

Some of the problems can be a result of faulty machines, old equipment, poor performance from the labor force and more. Whatever the problem is, it must be addressed. Timeliness is also a key factor when addressing the problem.

1. Checking for a Pulse

An organization showing signs of death must be checked for a pulse. This is often a regular practice in the medical field when a patient is in critical condition and needs urgent medical attention from medical personnel. It will be poor judgment, if not unwise, to administer medical attention to an organization that has died. Dead organizations do not need medical attention! Despite how expensive or good quality the medication is, dead organizations cannot make any use of such medical assistance.

Sometimes, businesses do not recognize that some or all parts of their organization are already dying since they are too busy seeking profits and looking at the competition.

Past performances should not be an indication of future outcomes. An organization must constantly assess itself and grow for the future.

1.1 Acknowledge that help is needed

Whenever an organization is experiencing challenges, it cannot operate as though everything is all right. This is an approach taken by some persons who have problems but do not want to tell anyone. Sometimes, when they decide to inform others, it is already too late.

Acknowledging that the organization needs help is important. When members of an organization are courageous enough to say that they are experiencing some challenges and that they need help, you will be surprised to see many persons coming to their rescue.

Those organizations that stand up and say that they need help will be provided with great support within a short time. However, those that choose to keep things to themselves may soon die or live in a state of disequilibrium.

1.2 Internal illness

Some of the pains of an organization are internal, and people may not know of them. Some internal pains are so strong that they can cause the organization to quickly die if they are not recognized and addressed immediately. When an organization hides its internal struggles, they may spread like cancer, in which they suddenly take over parts of its body (departments), and soon, many other parts that were operating properly will begin to show signs of deterioration.

An affected organization may sometimes not be able to properly address its internal problems. Therefore, it needs help or guidance. Also, some people get relief from their internal issues by telling them to someone else.

1.3 Skilled helper is needed

When there is a need to check for a pulse, especially when the organization is about to die, experienced and knowledgeable medical officer(s) (consultants) should be the ones to provide a diagnosis as amateurs sometimes cannot provide the urgent help needed.

When the organization is next to death's door, there is no time for play. Amateurs may take too long in trying to diagnose the issue(s). However, those that are mature and knowledgeable will quickly go to the area where the pulse is.

Remember that skilled medical practitioners are trained to find and check the pulse during emergency situations. They can also provide or recommend technical assistance you might not have considered.

The price to pay for skilled helpers may be a factor to consider. However, when an organization needs urgent help, the cost becomes a secondary issue. If an organization has enough family and friends, then someone may be willing to provide some financial assistance. However, there are organizations that fail to acknowledge the help and support they receive during tough situations. This bad practice has caused some organizations to not want to help other organizations that are dying.

1.4 Different parts of an organization

The pulse can be found in different parts of an organization. Often, some medical practitioners have a prejudice and believe that the pulse can only be found at a specific spot of an organization. When an organization shows signs of dying, the pulse is easy to identify. It must be noted that not all organizations may be diagnosed with the same illness; therefore, different parts of the organization have to be checked to find the pulse.

1.5 Where to search for the pulse

Medical practitioners spend some amount of time trying to find a pulse in an individual. Once the medical practitioner reaches the patient (organization), urgent action must be taken to find out which part of the organization still has life. Like in a living organism, at least one sign of life must be found, and then medical assistance will be provided. A medical practitioner can check some parts of the organization quickly. Different organizations may have different names for the same functions, and these functions do not necessarily operate in every organization.

Figure 1. Some of the main organs of an organization

(All figures are developed by the author unless otherwise noted.)

It might be important to check any or all of these departments to find a pulse. These departments are separate but are all important for the functioning of an organization. When one of these departments has an infection, the entire organization can be quickly affected. However, some do not understand that the entire body depends heavily on the effective functioning of all parts of the organization.

Some persons often consider some departments greater than others, but like in sickness, when one part of the body is affected, the entire body may become paralyzed. The same is true for an organization; if one department is affected, then the entire organization may be affected.

1.6 Screen off the organization and disaggregate its structures from its functions

In checking where the pulse is, screening off the organization is important to avoid distractions and onlookers. Several persons may share their opinions when the medical practitioner is looking for a pulse, distracting the medical practitioner. Sometimes finding a pulse is difficult and must be done quickly before the organization fails. Therefore, preventing those who may want to distract the rescue operation is important. Those within the encircled area should be persons who can offer some help or advice.

Oftentimes, too many persons have varying views, which delay the search for an important and urgent thing, the pulse. Some persons have mastered the art of providing suggestions that may cause some medical practitioner to be persuaded and to act differently from the routine medical training.

Less distraction can help find the pulse faster, with less energy exerted. Not all organizations that are about to die can wait while the medical practitioner takes time to find the pulse. Some may be about to take their last breath before a medical practitioner comes to the rescue. Therefore, immediate action is always needed when a medical practitioner is summoned to attend to such urgent matter.

If the organization is about to die, those who will be affected by its death should be considered. Therefore, every effort must be made to help a dying organization regain life, unless the organization is into illegal activities.

2. Identifying the Main Organs

The human body has many parts; however, only some of them are main organs.

In an organization, the medical practitioner must identify the main departments or functions that might have been affected. Once the main organ affected is known, then the medical practitioner's work becomes easier as greater attention can now be spent on addressing the main issue of that organization.

Sometimes some persons spend too much time on other organs that do not need urgent attention. When that happens, the dying organization may die quicker as the organ that needs the most attention is not attended to immediately.

2.1 People are human capital, support them

Every organ has an important function, same with every department. For some, some departments are less important. That may be right in their own eyes, but it may not be the truth. The absence of one department can cause many other departments to cease operations. For example, some persons do not see the janitorial service as important. However, if you let the janitor stay away from the job for at least two days, many persons within the organization will not be able to use the restrooms and have clean desks to work on, and the floor will be untidy, which may also lead to some accidents or injuries.

Too often, the classification of a person's importance is based on their own feelings. That feeling or myth may be far from the truth. Everyone is important in an organization, and everyone must be given importance.

When people and departments feel that other persons are treating them as less important, they start to disconnect, and then suddenly, this attitude spreads like cancer throughout the organization. Some people often only consider the major disease or things that can affect them. But sometimes, the little things can cause many other things to bring the body to a halt.

2.2 Identifying departments and their importance

Each department should be identified, as well as their importance. Some organizations have many departments, but others only have a few. Despite the number of departments, each of them has their own importance.

Once the importance of each department is identified, then care must be taken to treat that department with respect. Remember that if that department is not treated in a respectful manner, then the entire organization can be affected and soon may be in a dying state.

Once the department's importance is identified, choosing the key persons to lead the department to success is also important. On some occasions, it might be surprising to know that the head of the department may not be the one who is driving it to success. When the main persons or organs are identified, then their efforts must be acknowledged, and they must be treated with care. Some smart senior officers will try to have other persons learn from the important ones, so in the event that one person is not there, the organization will continue its normal operations.

Too many organizations depend on just a few individuals, and when they are absent, the organization is unable to function at optimal speed. That practice is dangerous and must be stopped immediately. All organizations should have different persons performing similar tasks. Though they may not be the best, they must be given an opportunity to learn and develop their skills.

For example, persons who are only right-handed or left-handed will mostly use that main hand. However, when they are put in a challenging position and need to use the other hand, they may encounter some problems. Since that is known, it is important to practice using the other hand as well to perform some functions so in the event of an emergency, that person may be able to deliver a reasonable planned result.

That same approach must be taken in an organization. Those parts or departments that are least used should be given the opportunity to be utilized more.

2.3 Burnout

Often, when one department is used and overused, it becomes burned out. Every department is expected to carry their weight. If too much burden is placed on one department, then the stresses of life can affect that department, and sudden sickness will become a permanent fixture for that department.

The organization may have many successes from one department, but efforts must be made to have every department taking on full responsibility since they were established to fulfill a specific function.

Overworked departments and people often collapse without any notice and may have to seek immediate medical attention. Those who are in-charge of departments constantly assess which department and persons are overworked. The solution to the problem will be to provide rest for that department or its members from time to time because if they are burned out, then the department's operations will suddenly be halted, and the entire organization will be affected.

Employees who are abused by organizations often seek ways of identifying they are overworked or seek to exit the organization. Some organizations have a high attrition rate, and their managements are not taking any appropriate action to remedy the situation.

High attrition rate can cause many organizations to suffer. Some of the external impact caused by high attrition are as follows:

- Decline in supply
- Delays in delivery of an expected product or service to customers
- Reduction of customers
- Increase in customer complaints

While these are only a few of the impacts of high attrition, a wise management team must think of solutions to these challenges. They may not have control over all the challenges, but efforts must be made to identify most of them, if not all, and then find possible short- and long-term solutions.

2.4 Identifying the critical departments

Like the human body, which has many important organs, the organization must identify which departments are important.

When the important organs are identified, then care must be exercised to prevent them from being affected and infected.

The main organs will remain important since it may be impossible to substitute their importance. Many persons in the organization should know what the main organs are and should try as often as possible to protect them. Due care must be exercised concerning them. The main organs must be put to work, but not to be overworked.

Some main organs are often abused by some organizations, and that is when they begin to malfunction, so attention must be given to them. In some situations, attention is provided too late as the organ might have been abused and in its last stage.

Every department is important, but some are critical. In rescuing the organization, attention must be paid quickly to the critical organs.

Organizations must also put preventive maintenance in place so that the critical departments are taken care of and not abused.

2.5 Some critical organs and their functions

Table 1. Some critical organs and their functions

Critical departments	Functions
Marketing	Aids in promoting the organization's products and services to potential customers
Procurement and Inventory	Seeks to acquire appropriate products and services for the organization
Manufacturing	Converts raw and semi finished materials into finished products
Finance and Account	Manages the organization's finances (inflows, outflows, investments, borrowings, costs, etc.)
Legal	Represents the organization on legal matters, drafts organization's legal agreements, etc.

Operation and Project	Manages the movement of people, products and services and ensures the projects are executed as planned

The table above lists some departments and gives a brief description of their functions. Some organizations may have other departments but are not mentioned in this table since every organization has different names for the same units.

Each unit is important to the organization, and if one fails, then the entire organization fails.

Sometimes, when trying to help someone, you have to find out what caused the problem. Knowing the cause will help in providing possible solutions.

3. Diagnosing the Cause of the Problem

Whenever a person takes their vehicle to the mechanic or service attendant for an emergency checkup, that person may have to answer several questions. The questions are not to intimidate the person, but to find out the root cause of the problem. Based on the information the person provides, the mechanic will then analyze it and probe to determine if the information provided is accurate and provide a remedy.

There are times that when the mechanic follows your advice concerning the problem, they may recognize that you did not provide accurate information, so they may proceed to other areas which could have caused the problem. At the end of the day, the mechanic will find the problem and provide the relief needed.

Now turn your attention to a human who is sick and is in a dying state. The paramedic or hospital may receive a call for emergency and may send an ambulance to provide some temporary assistance. On many occasions, the medical persons may have asked those that surround the persons what has caused the person to be in this dying state. They may also ask some important questions before they choose to administer medication or relief. The questions they ask are important in diagnosing the true cause of the problem and determining the appropriate measures.

This same approach of asking questions must be applied to organizations that are in a dying state. Questions must be asked before possible answers are provided. Some organizations may want to hide the truth of what has caused the organization to be in that state, but by hiding the truth, the organization may not receive the kind of help it needs.

Being real and truthful is often important to get the correct assistance. Help will be made available quickly to those who are honest enough to provide the correct information at the beginning.

Remember that anyone who is about to die may need your help. Your help may be just to be honest and to provide the correct information. A dying organization may not have the strength and courage to speak, so others may have to speak on its behalf.

Some organizations eliminate persons who are not honest and replace them with those who are honest and willing to speak the truth at the beginning. Some persons see that the organization is in a dying state but do not say anything. This practice sometimes occurs because some leaders do not want to take any advice. However, there are some leaders who would like to receive advice, but the employee is only concerned about their remuneration.

Every leader must ensure that he or she is surrounded with honest persons. The advice from honest persons may save the organization and prevent it from being in a dying state.

3.1 Conduct a surveillance survey

Those who want to rescue a dying organization must be willing and courageous enough to ask questions. The questions to be asked must only be the important ones since the organization is about to die soon if no help is offered.

The questions must not be to condemn the organization but to help it find a solution. Often, questions are asked to lay the blame on some persons for their actions. This is not acceptable when an organization is about to die. Finding out the problem and finding solutions must be the priority to revive the organization. When the organization is revived, then other appropriate actions can be taken to prevent the organization from falling into the same situation where a rescue team is needed again.

Most of the time, when an organization is about to die, a matured and experienced person is needed to ask the questions and provide the help needed. Some amateurs may have the correct questions but may not be able to carefully provide the help needed. When only one pulse is found, then time is against those who have to provide the help needed.

It might be important to ask the medical practitioner questions in a sequential manner. However, there are times that you may have to skip some sequences to address an urgent matter. Some persons are so rigid that they must follow the sequence they know. That approach may lead to the organization moving from a state of dying to death.

The questions to be asked must provide a lead toward the major issue that might have caused the organization to be in its current state.

3.2 Seek Organizational Development

After the questions have been asked and relevant information have been provided, it is time to provide the help that will cause the organization to live again. Many organizations want to live again, but someone must be there for them in moving from a dying state back to life.

Figure 2. If help is provided, then life can be restored

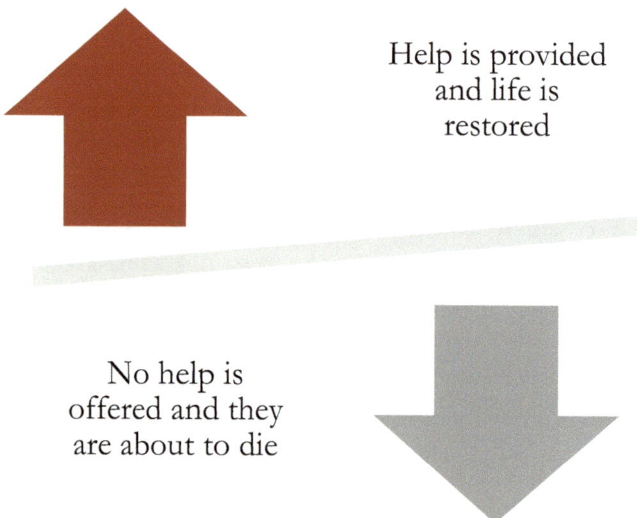

Finding a place that is most suited to provide the help needed is important. Not every part of the organization might be good to provide such help. There are some parts where once you find it and then provide the help, the rest of the body will quickly come alive.

The organization that needs help may be waiting for a quick injection of help. The help from one spot may ignite the whole organization. The organization has the ability to feed and take care of many persons. When this is known, then efforts must be made constantly to save many organizations that offer something good since many lives will be impacted from one organization.

The organization saved may, in turn, help those that saved it. Some aspects of life can have a cycle effect, where, when a person stretches out their hands to help, sometime in the future, the same organization that was helped will help many others, including those that directly helped it.

People should begin to look for ways of helping others and organizations as it may have a positive impact on the lives of many. Helping a dying organization may work in the favor of others, where they have helped themselves.

When the helper comes to the organization, they must be prepared in their minds that they can provide several assistances, but only one may be needed at that time. The right medication will produce the right results when administered at the right time.

Figure 3. Right results because of right medication

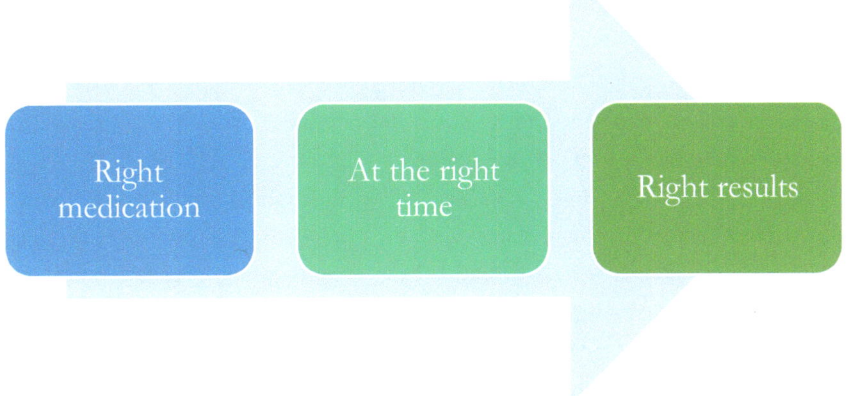

Not all people (including owners and managers) receiving help will remember to express thanks, but as a helper, you must not be discouraged because a thank-you was not expressed. Some organizations must be so happy to be alive that they forget to give thanks, but do not stop and just continue to do that what is right. That is, saving the lives of others.

Section 2. Relying on Experiential Learning

When an organization goes through a challenging moment, it is important that the management of that organization tries to learn from the past. Those that fail to do so may find themselves in the same situation again. The past is a good learning opportunity.

The pain from the past may remain in some organizations, and their reputation may be affected. Some customers may be lost in the process, but some new customers may also be gained.

It is important to have all organs working together. The reasons they might have had medical issues was because only one or a few of the organs were carrying most of the workload for the organization. This is a common problem, where just a few departments are doing most of the work. That might have been the past, but that cannot continue since the organization may once again be seeking medical attention. Teamwork is a key ingredient for the success of any organization. If your organization does not have teamwork, then now is the right time to practice it.

The problem must be removed. Harboring the problem may only allow the organization to experience the same issues again and again. Removing the problem may be problematic on some occasions, but it might be necessary. The successful removal of the problem may allow the organization to function effectively once again.

When some elements are removed, then something must be added. Employing people with the right skill sets are very important. People are a key resource who can lead the organization to success. If the people employed do not possess the right skill set, then they might contribute to the decline of the organization. Some organizations conduct trainings for their employees to assist with the success of the organization. Realignment of employees can also help. Finding quality persons is never an easy task.

When the right persons are found, assessing their performances and rewarding them appropriately are important. When an organization fail to recognize people's contributions, then the employee may choose another organization to share their skills and knowledge with. It is not always easy to find people who have the skills necessary for the success of the organization.

Employees must feel comfortable with the organization they work for. They must be given the scope to work and share their skills. When some persons are allowed to operate effectively in the organization, they may turn a problematic organization into a successful one. Organizations must work toward having people who can help rather than those who will destroy the organization.

4. All Organs Must Work Together at the Expected Speed

Once the good organs are found, then it is important to have them work together. When the pulse has been found and the organization is reviving, then efforts must be made to have the organs work as a team.

If only one department of an organization has to carry the workload of the entire organization, then soon the organization may find itself needing rescue efforts. The cause of collapse of an organization might have been because only one department is working.

Often, many departments do not carry out their full duties. The absence of their effort will suddenly cause many other departments to fail, and then the entire organization may soon need a rescue team.

4.1 Clear directions and mission for each department

It is important to prevent the organization from having a relapse. Therefore, the entire department should be provided with clear guidelines.

Sometimes, when an organization has recently started, there may not be clear requirements for each department. The organization is just beginning to grow, and persons may be too busy to establish clear guidelines. However, if this malpractice continues for a prolonged period, then it will lead toward confusion and challenges.

Creating clear boundaries and requirements for each department will help the organization to achieve success, and every department will contribute to such success. Organizations that are well-aligned and have skilled persons delivering the desired results have higher chances of success.

4.2 Performance review

The targets set for each department must be reviewed. The review must be done at an established timeline. The targets set must be SMART

(Specific, Measurable, Achievable, Relevant, Time Bound). Without measurable targets, then the organization may not achieve its goals.

If a performance review is not conducted on a regular basis, then some departments may continue to produce results which are below par and cause other departments to carry additional duties.

If some departments' performances are found to be lacking, then some amount of corrective actions must be taken. Those departments that recognize that sanctions will be instituted will quickly understand that they have to constantly work toward delivering high-level performances.

Some organizations have linked the senior manager remuneration to the performance of their department. When this approach is taken, it is important to only measure managers in those areas which they have control over. There are controllable and uncontrollable areas of operation. For example, no human being has control over the weather. Therefore, if the performance of the manager will be severely affected by weather, then there must be room to consider or eliminate its effect from their performance.

The performance management system must not affect the individual but help them to see what has happened and how they can improve. There must also be adequate reporting systems allowing for easy access of the required information. Where it might be possible, the time and format for reporting must be consistent and system generated.

Regular feedbacks must be provided once the individual, department and organization are assessed. The feedback must allow for corrective actions. In some organizations, people hate feedbacks that will ask them to take corrective action. Their refusal to act on feedback might cause their decline.

4.3 Strong team

When the team is strong, the organization is expected to accomplish many of the tasks set before it. Those who are responsible for setting targets must set realistic ones. If the targets are out of the reach of the employees, then they may not put in any effort to try to reach them since they know that the targets are unrealistic.

A strong team can produce dynamic results. It is often surprising to see how many things can be accomplished when people and departments work together.

If you want to see failure, then get people and department to fight against each other. On the contrary, if you want people and departments to have great success, then get them to work together.

A divided team will not yield success. A united team will. Therefore, having people and departments working together is advisable.

4.3.1 What is a team?

The project team comprises people with assigned roles and responsibilities for completing the project (PMBOK 4, 2008).

Building a strong team is necessary to aid in the organization's success. Oftentimes, poor team performance contributes to the decline of an organization.

The ability to motivate others is a fundamental leadership skill and has strong connections to building cohesive and goal-oriented teams and getting results through others (Hughes et al., 2014).

4.4 Characteristics of a team

Group cohesion is the glue that keeps a group together. It is the sum of the forces that attract members to a group, provide resistance to leaving it and motivate them to be active in it (Hughes et al., 2015).

Table 2. Variables for team effectiveness

Variables	Explanation
Task	Does the team know its tasks? Does the team have a meaningful piece of the work, sufficient autonomy to perform it and access to knowledge of its results?
Boundaries	Is the collective membership of the team appropriate for the task to be performed? In addition to task skills, does the team have sufficient maturity and interpersonal skills to be able to work together and resolve conflicts?
Norms	Does the team share an appropriate set of norms for working as a team? If the team is to have a strategy that works

	overtime, do conflicting norms not confuse team members?
Authority	Has the leader established a climate where authority can be used in a flexible rather than a rigid manner? Do team members feel comfortable in questioning the leader on decisions where there are no clear right answers?

(Extracted from Hughes et al., 2015, p. 413)

4.5 Stages in team development

All groups must go through various stages. Some of the stages may be common, and others may vary to some persons. When the team is established to help the organization, despite being experienced in their own professional capacity, they may go through these stages.

Table 3. Group development stages

Forming	The gathering of superficial information about fellow members and low trust
Storming	Usually marked by intragroup conflict, heightened emotional levels and status differentiation as remaining contenders struggle to build alliances and fulfill the group's leadership role
Norming	The clear emergence of a leader and development of group norms and cohesiveness are the key indicators of the norming stage of group development.
Performing	Group members play functional, interdependent roles that are focused on the performance of the group tasks.

(Extracted from Hughes, et al., 2016, p. 397)

Because many conflicts are the result of misunderstandings and communication breakdowns, leaders can minimize the level of conflict within and between groups by improving their communication and listening skills, as well as spending time networking with others (Hughes et al., 2014).

Team ground rules, group norms and solid project management practices like communication planning and role definition reduce the amount of conflict (PMBOK, 2008).

Getting the team to work as one is never an easy task. Much effort will have to be exercised, and some amount of patience is needed to help persons to become one.

A leader will have to demonstrate many skills of moving persons from an individual level to becoming a team. The early stage of blending persons together is never easy as each individual will try to maintain their individual identity, but that will not work in the interest of the organization.

Some organizations are unable to meet its target because people are not willing to put aside their differences and work together.

5. Removing the Problems

Part of the success of the organization in the future is to identify the problem and to find solutions. If the problem still exists, then the organization may find itself in the same situation where it will need to be rescued. The rescue operation may not work on all occasions. Therefore, it is important to find the problem and remove it.

5.1 Willingness and ability to remove the problem

Those in the organization must be willing to remove the issues affecting the organization. In life, if a person is affected by a particular illness, then the doctor must find out what caused that illness and remedy the situation. In the life of the organization, the problem identified must be carefully addressed.

Sometimes, it may be painful to remove some of the issues as they may affect some resources which are important to some parts of the organization. One key resource which is sometimes overlooked is the human capital. When some persons joined the organization, their contribution might have been outstanding; however, because they have become familiar with the task, they have failed to improve.

When the job becomes mundane, then people can lose their focus, and their performance begins to decline. Such decline sometimes affect the overall performance of the organization, causing it to need rescue.

People can be of great help to an organization. However, if they are not monitored, then their performance may decline, which will have an adverse effect on the organization.

With modern technology, some performances by the human capital may become redundant or less needed. The organization must be willing to decide on the amount and type of human capital needed for its operation.

Too many persons without adequate workload may be a significant cost to the organization without any return.

Training is important for the success of the human capital. Work is changing regularly. Those who have been employed for many years may need some amount of retraining. Training must not be seen as a challenge, but rather a learning opportunity to enhance their skills and knowledge.

5.2 Old and damaged machines

Another area in which the problem may exist is old and damaged machines. When machines are newly acquired, they are able to deliver maximum results. But they must be maintained. Sometimes, the maintenance costs are huge, and may organizations try to avoid them.

When organizations are having financial challenges, there may be the need to prioritize its financial needs. Adequate financing for an organization can bring much relief. On the contrary, lack of finance can bring much challenge to those who have to manage the organization.

Figure 4. The success and pitfall of the finances of an organization

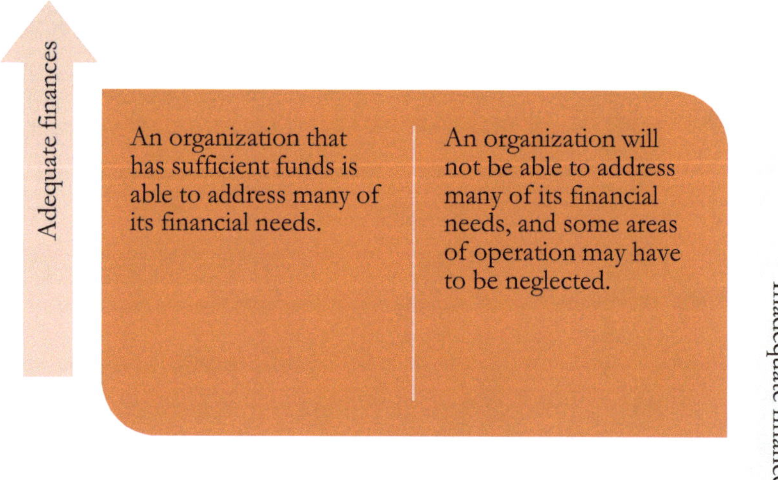

Some machinery may be critical for the effective functioning of the organization. However, the lack of funds will cause the organization to incur a loss by not having enough revenues to offset the costs.

For many aspects of businesses, the cost can be either be fixed or variable cost, which is explained in the table below.

Table 4. Costs and their definitions

Key terms	Meaning
Fixed cost	Is a cost which is incurred for a particular period of time and which, within certain activity levels, is unaffected by changes in the level of activity
Variable cost	Is a cost which tends to vary with the level of activity
Product cost	Are costs identified with the finished product

(Extracted from ACCA, CAT, B2, 1997)

Efforts must also be exercised to monitor both fixed and variable cost. Variable cost, if not properly monitored, can continue to increase and may cause the organization to move from a profit-making position to a loss-making position. One such cost is employment cost.

While rental of office space (rental of building) is a fixed cost, organizations must make maximum use of every possible space available to them.

5.3 Direct and indirect costs

An organization can further split the costs into two cost elements (ACCA, CAT B2, 1997), that is, direct and indirect costs as shown below.

Figure 5. Direct and indirect costs

Materials	Labour	Expenses
• Direct material • Indirect material	• Direct labor • Indirect Labor	• Direct expenses • Indirect expenses

(Extracted from ACCA, CAT, B2, 1997)

Old and damaged machines can continue to increase the cost to an organization. If an organization does not pay much attention to these increasing costs, then the organization can move from a position of profit to one of loss.

Those who are placed in charge of managing the affairs of the organization (principals and agents) must constantly look for areas where costs may be increasing. Whenever there is a fixed cost, the organization must make enough effort to generate revenues which will surpass such fixed cost. Too many fixed costs may result in the organization expending monies without having any benefit.

5.4 Replacements

If the human capital and machinery are not functioning properly, then it might be time to replace such resources.

With the replacement of resources, the organization may move quickly from a state of needing rescue to a state of health and vitality. Replacement has its cost, but the rewards can be greater. Those who are responsible for the replacement must ensure that proper assessments are done before implementation.

There may be situations where some of the replacements can be done in a phased approach, while on other occasions, they may have to be done in a block or complete set. The cost for the replacement must always be carefully considered.

5.5 Costs and benefits

Organizations are often bothered about the cost, but they must be willing to think of the future and consider the benefits. Whenever an investment has to be done, there must be a cost–benefit analysis.

When organizations are only concerned about the costs, then they may not see the benefits. If the benefits outweigh the costs, then the investment is worth the while.

The cost will include all monies which have to be expended to have the item or service. However, the benefits will include all of the success and achievements the organization will have at its disposal once the investment is made.

6. Employing the Right People (Multiskilled People)

In the earlier chapter, it was learned that people can be a problem toward the success of an organization. However, in this chapter, you will learn that people can help the organization to be successful.

Training is a planned effort to facilitate the learning of job-related knowledge, skills and behavior by employees (Noe et al., 2015).

Some organizations need many persons to help them deliver the required results. For some schools, an adequate number of teachers is needed to help the children learn. For some countries, the military force may require a large amount of people. People can be a good resource for the organization's success.

Large amounts of people can be helpful and disadvantageous at the same time. Managing people is a very important aspect to utilize the skills that people have. Some individuals are able to work independently, while others need direct supervision. Direct supervision provides a clear direction to those who might not be able to provide answers or solutions to some concerns.

Not everyone in the organization might be able to generate ideas which are appropriate. Some persons have worked a long time with the organization but are still unable to produce answers to the changing situations.

6.1 Employ fit and proper persons

Part of the success of the organization is to have people who will deliver the required results. These individuals must be "fit and proper". The individual chosen must have the knowledge, experience and soft skills.

Too often, people who are employed only have one of those key ingredients. Academic persons want to treat the organization like a classroom or submitting a technical document. However, the success of the organization will require persons who will be able to move from book knowledge to assisting the organization to grow. This may require such individual to be actually involved in the operation of the department or organization. Some leaders are able to provide technical knowledge but unable to do the actual work.

You may know those officers who are unable to do the work as they may often have difficulty to complete any task. If the key staffs are not available, the leader may not be able to do everything, but he/she must be in a position to perform certain tasks.

The fit and proper person chosen must be willing to work and be a team player. Some persons are often happy to work alone, but that approach must not become the norm. Working together will allow organizations to gain greater successes rather than each individual working separately. Having some people working alone might have caused the organization to be in a dying state.

It is expected that those who work in the organization possess soft skills. They must be able to jell together, share ideas, have social interactions, use software, etc. When employees are able to get along with each other, tensions are avoided.

An organization needs people who have the passion for the growth of the organization. Some may have other motives when they work with an organization, but their overall goal must be to help the organization. When the team has a shared mind-set and is willing to work together, then the organization will be able to realize its goal.

The organization must work with its human capital constantly for the effective delivery of its plans and programs which have been outlined for each period. The human capital of any organization may contribute to its failure or success. With quality leaders guiding the employees, the results may be outstanding. Each leader may influence the employee to do either good or bad.

Figure 6. Effects of influence on the lives of people

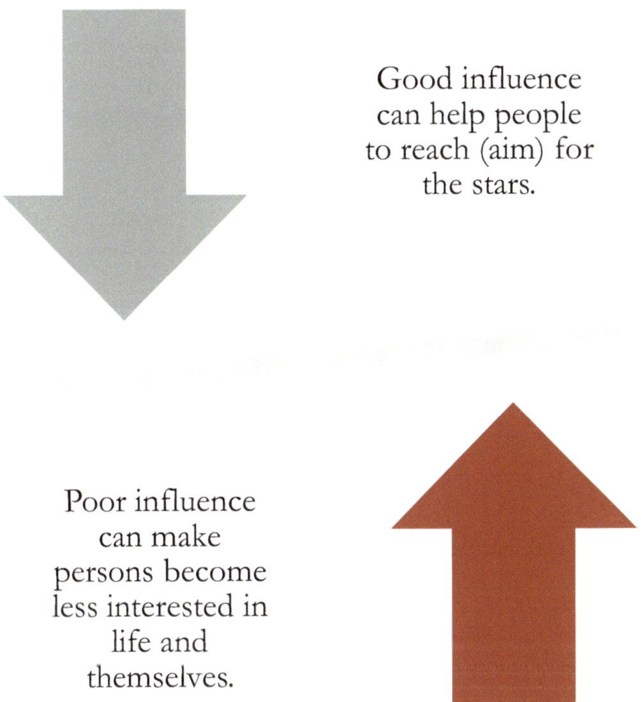

6.2 Training

An employee may join the organization with much skill and academics, but is that employee ready for that organization? It cannot be overemphasized that each organization has something unique about it. The persons who join the organization may have many great ambitions, but the organization has its own system and culture. Therefore, they must be familiar with it. Once the individual knows what is expected from them, they spend less time fighting (or addressing conflict) and spend more time doing productive work.

Many organizations are happier to spend time on productive work rather than addressing conflicts. Conflict is like a poison. If it is not addressed quickly, it can kill the person whom it comes into contact with. Some conflicts are akin to deadly snakes, that it only needs one strike at you, and you will be pronounced dead within seconds.

Figure 7. Training helps

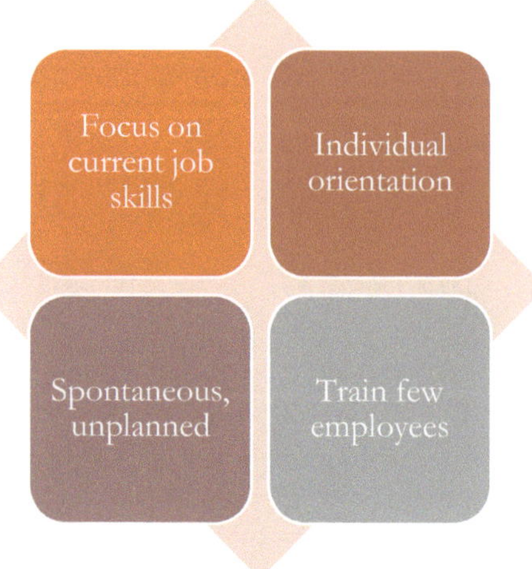

(Developed from Noe et al., 2015)

Training is important for employees of all organizations. Even if some persons are "fit and proper" for the job, they will still need some amount of training. But the training provided will vary in intensity. Some persons are quick learners, while others may need some time to be taught and to digest the information and may need some hand-holding session until they feel comfortable to deliver the desired results.

Training often equips a person for the task ahead of them. It can be provided at the initial stage of the person's employment or sometime later during the course of their work. Those responsible for new recruits will decide when training is appropriate. Some organizations have a standard policy on who must be trained, when training will be administered, how frequent, if the training will be done in the classroom or at your desks, etc.

Whether there is a structured way of providing training or an ad hoc approach, the organization should ensure persons are trained. A trained and experienced workforce is a key component the organization needs for its success. Some organizations have made it their policy to ensure staff are trained and those who are trained are provided with some incentive to retain them. Many organizations see their human capital as a key resource toward their success and will try very hard to retain their employees. This is a strategic move, and such view must be embraced by all senior officers within the organization.

The challenge some organizations face, which leads to its decline, is the belief that once an employee has been trained once, then that employee does not have to be retrained. It must be noted that sometimes the best people do not deliver the results that are expected of them.

If there are persons who are excellent in their performance and are consistent, then such individuals can be used to provide further training to others or used as a coach, role model, etc.

Some organizations do not use its own resources and incur additional costs to request the service of a person to provide training, which could have been easily done by an existing employee.

If an existing employee is used to provide such training, then the senior management team must also agree on the content of the information if they have some background knowledge and help support the training officer. Sharing knowledge is good. Those who know must train others to help those who do not. With more persons able to perform the same task, then the organization can have constant and high-level success.

Employees must remember that if they fail to deliver what they are tasked to do, then the organization may fail. However, if the employee does their best, then the organization may have the success it needs.

Figure 8. Employees who are trained can enhance the organization's profit

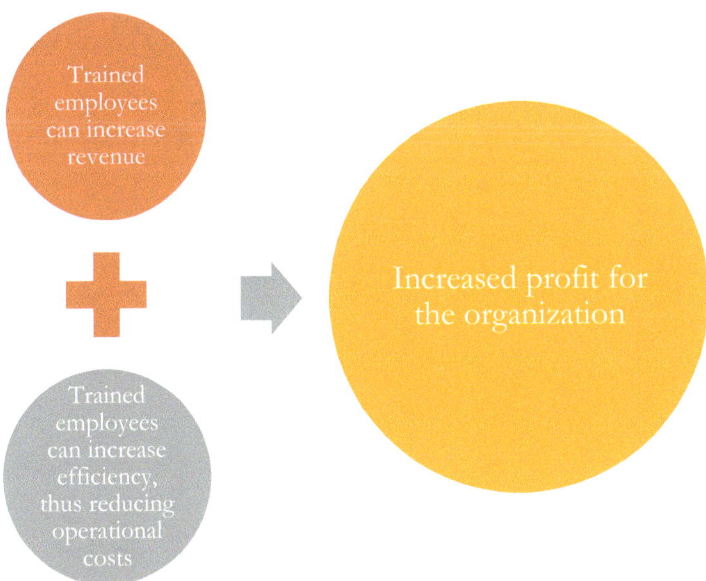

More employees need to deliver their best and help the organization to become successful. The organization must also compensate the employees for the work they have done. Some employees leave an organization because of poor working conditions and inadequate compensation.

Organizations must allocate a budget for training so that they will have persons who are knowledgeable and skilled to help them succeeds. Training must not be a one-off event, but must be continuous, and it should be done for different aspects of the organization.

Figure 9. Training existing and new employees

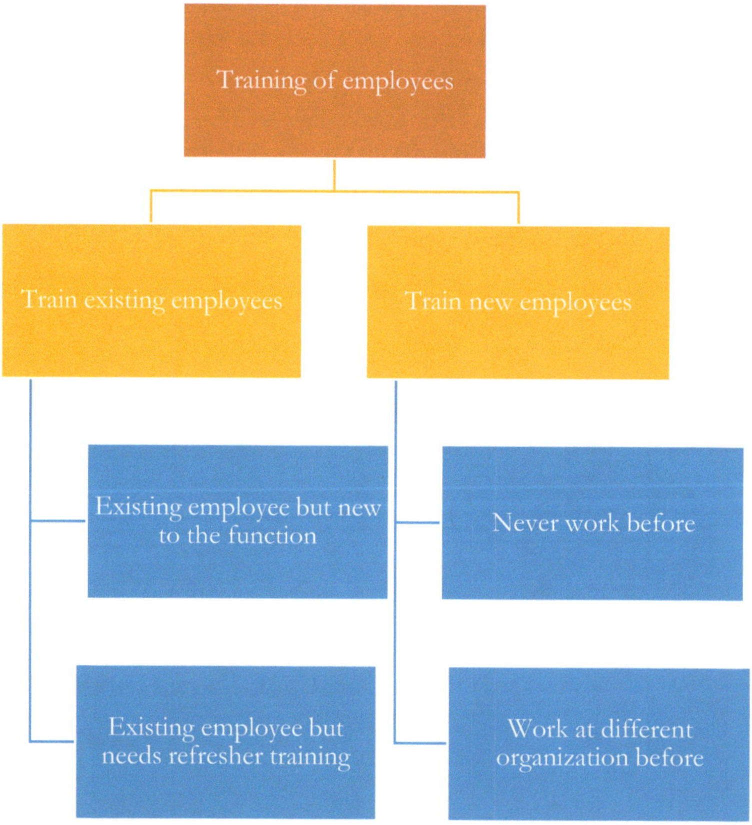

Training costs can be a significant portion of the organization's budget, so they must be monitored and managed. Trained employees should also be provided with opportunities to exercise what they have learned.

The organization ought to provide training, but the training costs must not escalate, and efforts must be made to reduce such costs.

Figure 10. Ways to reduce training costs

Train many employees at once

Document process or procedure of how tasks are to be completed

Establish manual for tasks

Engage each person within each department to train at least one person in that department

Implement job rotation

Upload recent training video, manual, etc., on the intranet, website, or social media

Recruit highly skilled and experience staff within the same industry or who operate in the same position

6.3 Development

Training is good, but the organization must be deliberate concerning the development of its employees. Many organizations feel one-off training will allow the organization to deliver its desired results. If this is the view of some organizations, then this might have led to their failure.

Development is the acquisition of knowledge, skills and behaviors that improve an employee's ability to meet changes in job requirements and client and customer demands (Noe et al., 2015).

People need constant sessions to learn. With regular sessions, they become proficient in what they need to do.

When an organization decides to develop its employees, it will later experience its impact.

Knowledge and information are constantly changing. Those who are able to receive additional knowledge and exposure can better withstand the challenges of life. Many years ago, some aspects of business and operation remained the same. But with the advanced technology and artificial intelligence, many things have changed. The way persons are expected to receive messages from an organization has changed with the advent of many technological devices.

People can now conduct many of their businesses without leaving the comfort of their home. The organization must also help its employees improve so that they can meet such changing demands.

Figure 11. Importance of development for organizational success

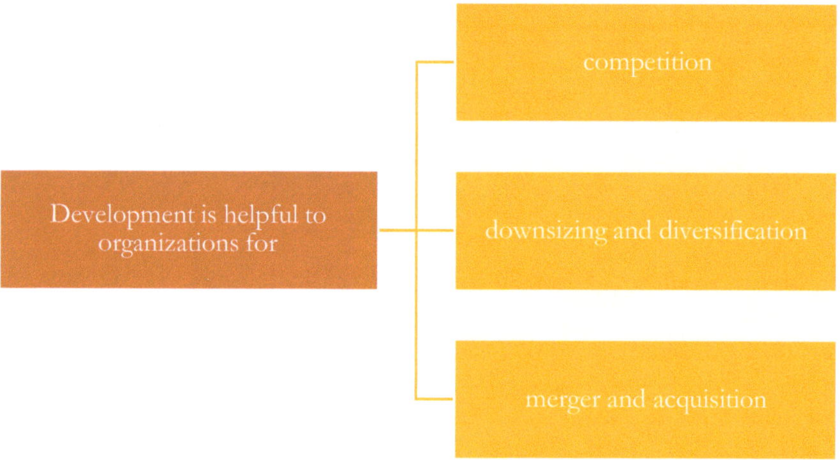

Organizations should not wait and hope for employees to invest in their own development. If they choose to increase their knowledge or skills, they may quickly look for an opportunity to exit the business, where their additional skills and knowledge will be properly compensated for.

The development of employees will help the organization to be competitive and will assist when there is a merger and diversification. Besides the acquisition of machinery and advanced technology, there is a great need to help employees develop.

Competition will continue to increase, but sometimes, those employees that the organization invest in will help the organization face all challenges and remain competitive.

Organizations must include funds for development in their annual budget.

Figure 12. Development helps

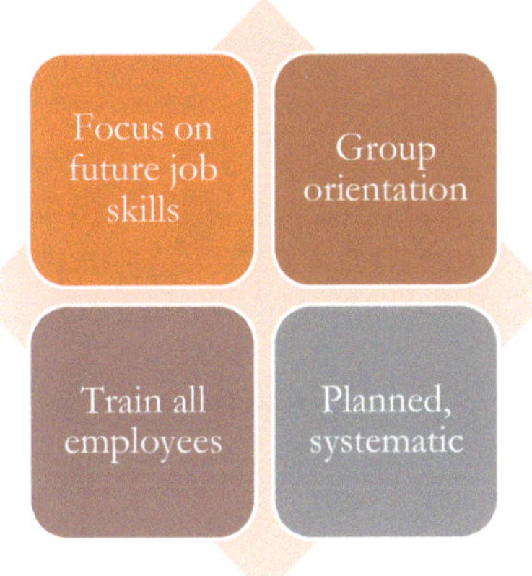

(Developed from Noe et al., 2015)

These funds for development must be linked to a proper development program, which will help the employees become better. The development program should include many areas and, if possible, many employees. The entire organization must work as a team, and as many persons are exposed to development, the entire organization will grow.

Some organizations die because only a few persons, sometimes only the favorite employees, are sent on development programs, while those who are not favored will not be provided with any opportunity for development. Development must never be bias. The organization needs all its employees for its success, despite their status in the organization.

Figure 13. Approaches to employee development

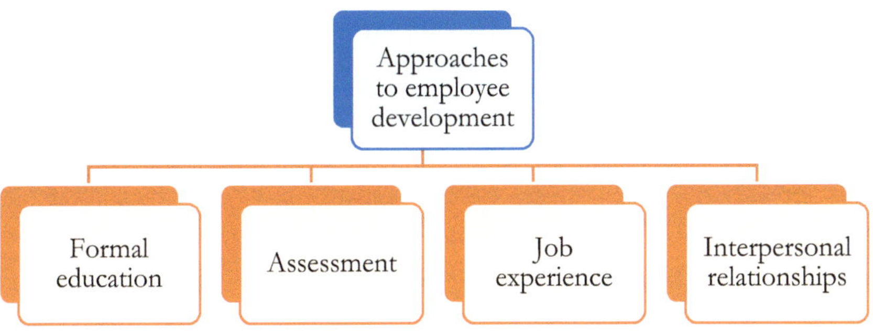

(Developed from Noe et al., 2015)

7. Performance Appraisal

An organization that employs quality persons cannot leave them to work forever without assessing their performance. Even the best machine or equipment should be assessed. Part of the failure of some organizations is tied to the fact that they employ quality people and acquire quality machines but fail to assess their performance in the future.

Some have a tendency of underperforming if their performances are not measured and no feedback is provided. When people have been working in an organization for a long time, they learn many "shortcuts". These shortcuts work for them, but not necessarily for the organization. The organization thinks that they are getting their desired outcomes but fails to recognize that some of the processes are not being followed.

Some organizations have increased their performance, but when a proper assessment is done, some employees are found to be practicing some things that the organization does not embrace. Here are some issues that some organizations may encounter if careful and regular assessment is not done:

- Child labor, where underage children are working for the organization directly or indirectly
- Employees working longer hours than the labor laws require and are not properly compensated and sometimes do not have the required protective clothing
- Purchase of lower standard items to be used in the input process

While an organization may achieve success because of the practices mentioned above, such success is disadvantageous to its future, and the practices might be the reason for its death since many lawsuits could be imposed on the organization.

In considering the assessment of employees' performance, think of it as a parent–child relationship. Some children will only do the right things when their parents are monitoring them, while others who are often obedient may require little supervision. However, as the management of the organization, you will not be able to assess all employees based on observation. Therefore, a formal assessment of their performance is necessary.

Once formal assessments are done, then the management of the organization will be able to acknowledge those who have done the required things and encourage those that have not delivered according to expectations. A group may also be told that the organization no longer needs their services.

Those people who manage an organization should not be afraid to assess the performance of its employees since that assessment will allow them to find out what may have caused the organization to fail and what can be done to make it successful.

Feedback is important when assessing employees. Some employees complain that they were assessed but did not receive feedback. Employers must be willing to provide feedback and a listening ear to their employees. Those who listen to their employees will be able to find some workable solutions for their organization's success.

It is often encouraging to know that the success of some organizations is known by the employees, but some do not listen to their employees and choose to take decisions that will not work well for them.

Often, a compromise is needed if the organization is to go forward.

The management of the organization must not conduct an assessment only when the employee has done something that the management deems incorrect. Assessments must be done in a structured manner at a prescribed time.

The assessment of employees must not be an emotional exercise but must remain professional and practicable. This approach may safeguard against some persons being favored over another. It also reduces incidents of unethical feedback which are so often known to happen when employees inform of other persons who are mistreated during the assessment period.

7.1 Reward and recognition

Organizations can employ several people with the right skills and experiences they need, but they have a great responsibility to each employee for the future. Employees often expect to be recognized for their outstanding performance and look for a reward after working hard for an organization. Again, it cannot be emphasized enough that some organizations are dying or die because they failed to reward their employees.

When employees know that their skills and knowledge can be better compensated, they look for another environment to be better appreciated. But not all employees are looking for additional monies. Some expect to be treated better and want certain benefits to be available to them.

People are not machines. Therefore, they should be treated with respect and love and should be rewarded. If an employee knows that they will be rewarded sometime in the future for their efforts, then they may use their energies and wisdom in helping the organization to be successful.

When the employees know that the organization does not and will not recognize their contribution or reward them, they will perform on the job as they deem necessary based on the treatment of the organization. This can be challenging for the organization since they may miss the opportunity of becoming one of the most profitable businesses within their industry, if only the employees were recognized and rewarded.

When an organization is considering giving rewards to its employees, they can use the table below to guide their decision-making.

Table 5. Components of "total reward"

Extrinsic rewards	
Fixed rewards of remuneration	<ul><li>Fixed or base pay</li><li>Cash benefits</li><li>Performance-related pay</li></ul>
Development rewards	<ul><li>Learning, training and development</li><li>Succession planning</li><li>Career progression</li><li>Other indirect or noncash benefits</li></ul>
Social rewards	<ul><li>Organizational climate or management culture</li><li>Performance support</li><li>Work group affinity</li></ul>

• Work-life balance • Other indirect or noncash benefits
Intrinsic rewards
• Job challenge • Responsibility • Autonomy • Task variety

(Extracted from Shields et al., 2016)

Some organizations should be congratulated for their efforts and contributions to employees. They often look for ways of recognizing their employees and, on some occasions, reward them, where practicable. When animals and people feel appreciated by someone, they are willing to cling to that person because they feel as though they are loved and treated with some amount of dignity.

Most remuneration packages will involve these components shown below.

Figure 14. Remuneration components

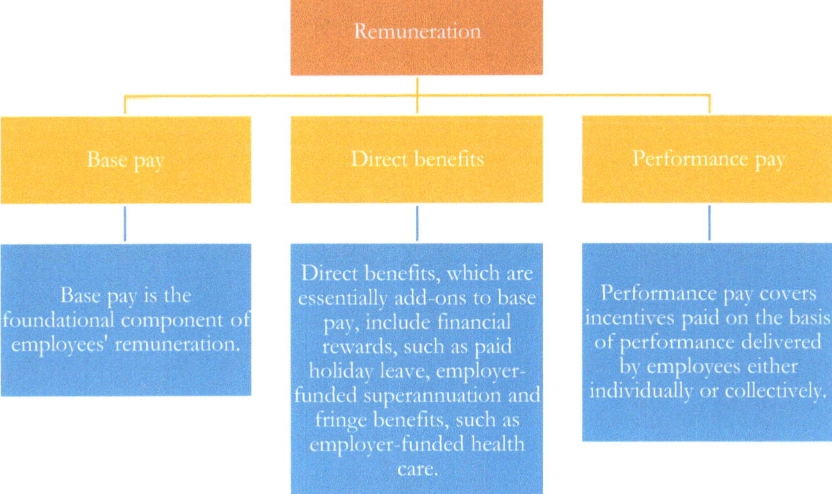

(Extracted from Shields et al., 2016)

Section 3. Fully Recovered

After a long and intense effort, the organization might be able to find its way back on the road of recovery. Any organization which has recovered will be more than happy to stay alive. To be alive is a good thing!

Those organizations that have been successful from the rescue operation would like to make success a daily diet. They will do everything to stay alive. Staying alive can be very challenging, but it is better than being dead.

A successful organization, which has survived the rescue, will have to work toward building muscles. It should establish itself and spread its operations. When the operations are spread, the organization can minimize some of the risks which are common to other organizations. Having a new customer base is important as it will guarantee additional revenues.

The success of an organization against the challenges of life serves as a learning experience for other organizations to follow. Sharing its challenges and success with selected and confidential persons may be a good medicine to prevent other organizations from falling into the same situation. However, some persons are selfish and do not want to share what has happened to their organization. They see others going into the same direction of failure without warning them.

Success is good, but trying to improve should be a constant desire for each organization. You can have incremental improvements or dynamic success because of the changes. An organization should not plan to stay where it is forever but try to improve regularly.

Planning for the future requires much foresight. The future is not guaranteed to anyone, but planning for it helps us to grow. Always try to be conservative when planning for the future. Stick to your plan if most of the factors remain the same. If some factors change, then you will be required to make the necessary changes.

Often, the success of an organization requires the guidance of a visionary captain. Many times, there is success ahead, but not everyone is able to see it. A visionary captain can see far beyond that of other members of the organization.

You should connect with the public. Many persons may be depending on you. Marketing is an area that some organizations do not place much emphasis on, but that should change. Advertising what you have will allow your organization to meet more customers, gain more revenues and stay alive. When people know about the quality products you have, they may be willing to leave where they are and purchase what you have to offer. You should make the public familiar with what you have.

8. Building Muscles and Strength

Once the organization is able to weather the storm and move beyond the state of dying to a state of full recovery as strength has been regained, then the organization needs to find ways to build muscles.

Often, the management of the organization becomes comfortable that they have been rescued and can now breathe again. That may be a good sign for anyone who has been rescued, but the life of an organization is more than just living from day to day.

8.1 Building a new customer base

Moving beyond leaving the hospital after a rescue operation should not be about making up time, but rather making an impact!

Some organizations see customers as ordinary people whom they will use just to gain revenue. If that is the mentality of the organization, then customers will come and go. Customers should be seen as much more than revenue providers. If customers are treated well and taken care of, they may want to stay with that organization.

Customers like to be treated special. Therefore, organizations should make them feel that way. Before a customer walks through the door of an organization, they should feel a sense of belonging. If customers are treated kindly, they may return to the organization many times after and may even become loyal to the organization.

Customers do not become loyal to an organization overnight. They take some time to assess an organization and decide whether they want to stay with that organization. They have many reasons why they become loyal to an organization. Some organizations are skillful at making customers loyal to them. They intentionally plan for it and are willing to meet the needs of the customers to facilitate the process of building loyalty. Other organizations should follow in a similar pattern.

When customers become loyal to an organization, they may want to spend most of their money at that organization or provide support to it in the form of shorter credit terms if they have a need to which that organization can help with. Some customers are so loyal to some organizations that even if the item is out of stock, they will wait until that organization has the item. They proudly tell friends and families that they only shop from a particular store or organization whenever they need a particular item. They may also boast and tell others that most of their clothes and furniture are purchased from a particular organization or their organization only procures items from a particular organization.

Any organization that has loyal customers should ensure to keep such customers as they can be an asset to them. Many organizations have high advertising and marketing costs, and they will want to reduce those costs if they can have loyal customers. Maintaining customers has always been a low-cost exercise compared with looking for new ones. When new customers become attached to an organization, there is no guarantee that those customers will stay.

Organizations have seen the need to invest in customers, and some have provided them with loyalty cards and other special arrangements. Those loyalty cards are sometimes entitled to bonus points which will allow customers to shop at the organization and pay less than a first-time customer.

An organization should also keep a database of its customers. From the data stored in the customer database, the organization can decide what marketing strategy they can use to attract certain customers. Customers are sometimes surprised to know how the organization knows so much about them and how it is able to help them with bargains. The customer database, if used properly, can be a great tool in the hands of any organization. It must be properly constructed to deliver quick and accurate information about customers, which the organization can use to its advantage to generate the needed revenue.

8.2 Saving and increasing revenues

When an organization has recovered, it should make an effort to have some monies set aside. Not all the monies an organization receives should be consumed. Some organizations have the habit of consuming most, if not all, of the revenues generated. When this happens, the organization may soon find itself in a position where it may have to borrow monies to settle expenditures.

Borrowing may be good, but it is not always the best thing. Some organizations which are not disciplined may find itself in a situation where it is unable to repay persons or financial institutions and may have to close the business. When an organization chooses to borrow, much of the organization's personal information have to be shared with the borrower. At the initial stage, borrowing may be necessary for some organizations. This can also happen when an organization wants to engage in major capital projects or expansions. However, borrowing must not become the norm for any organization.

An organization that wants to be financially independent but is experiencing financial drought should increase its revenues, reduce its expenditures and have savings.

Figure 15. Making your organization financially strong

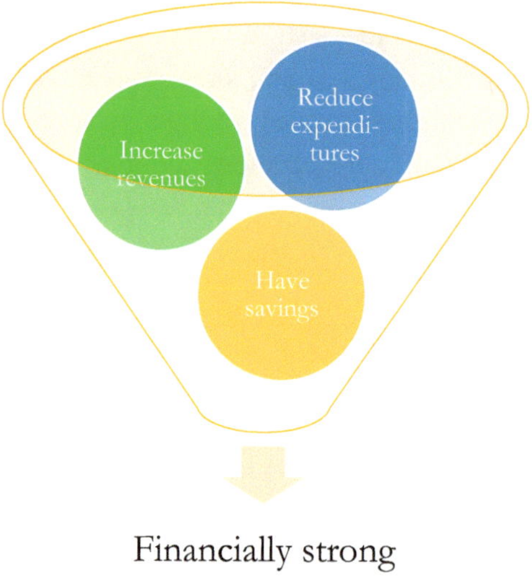

Financially strong

Some organizations choose to establish long-term and short-term savings. But before considering long-term savings, an organization should be able to take care of short-term expenditures first. Savings should be done using an interest-bearing account. The additional revenues generated from savings might be able to offset certain expenditures the organization will incur.

An organization should try to increase its revenues often. This may not always be an easy challenge, but profit-making organizations should work toward maximizing their revenues. When an organization is able to gain increased revenues, it may have an advantage over other organizations and may soon have the wherewithal to make further investments, which may quickly enhance the organization. Making additional revenues will help increase the market shares of an organization.

Put some monies in the bank now and gain some interest later! That should be the approach for many organizations. Keep a savings account for excess funds to be placed into that account so that the organization will be able to gain interest in the future.

The financial institution that the organization wants to establish a savings account with should be properly assessed since one would not want to lose their monies to a financial institution that will soon be closed because of poor management and lack of adherence to financial regulations.

8.3 Making profits, not losses

A strong organization should not only increase revenues but also make profits. Once there is an increase on the "bottom line," then many principals will be happy. This is an important indicator that the organization is making profits. It is surprising that some organizations have significant revenues but are unable to make profit. They get caught up with the revenue made and cannot maximize the profits. Making profit is not all about the amount of revenues but also the ability to carefully manage the financial resources available to the organization. If the expenditures exceed the revenues, then the organization will incur a loss.

Figure 16. Making an organization profitable

Organizations that are making profits should reserve some of their profits for future developments. Reserved profits can save an organization from future financial burdens.

Every organization must seek to increase its profits. This may be a challenge, especially with increasing competition. However, strong organizations will develop marketing plans to increase their revenues. Once the organization implements adequate cost reduction approaches, then there will be profits to be realized.

An organization may not make profit every day. However, when it does, it should note the strategies it used so that the same could be followed in the future. While an organization wants to make a profit so that it will have savings and be able to invest, it should not surcharge its customers. Some organizations want to make profit quicker than expected, but that may not be the best approach. Organizations should be careful in establishing its pricing strategy. A small and steady profit will allow the organization to operate for many years to come. Trying to make profit all at once may lead to the immediate death of the organization.

8.4 Investments in resources (people, machinery, treasury bills, etc.)

When profits and cash flows are realized, the organization should not consume all of them on short-term activities. When it wants to build muscles, it must remember that it has to invest in other resources such as people, machinery, savings accounts, etc.

For example, if a farmer plants his or her crops and sells or consumes all the products, then the question of what will be available for another season of planting is raised. This may be a similar situation that has caused some organizations to lose the financial resources needed for the future. When they finish harvesting the produce from the plantation, they consume most, if not all, or sell them.

Some successful organizations today have made the necessary investments, which provided them with the benefits they have now. If your organization adopts a similar approach, then it will continue in operation for a long time.

An organization should be willing to invest in its people. Some employees complain that their organization is only interested in making profits. When this happens, the organization does not see their employees as a resource to invest in but only see them for what they can get out of them. Employees who feel that their organization does not care about them will try to look for ways to get out of it and do not mind engaging in illegal or dangerous activities.

Organizations must be willing to invest in its people by ensuring the following:

- Employees are properly compensated.
- Tools, machinery and equipment are available for use.
- Training is provided.
- Development plans are implemented.
- Soft loans are offered, if possible, but adequate security and screenings should be put in place before lending.
- Transportation is available, if it is practicable.
- Medical benefits are enjoyed by all employees, as well as a pension scheme.

An organization should also invest in properties, plant and equipment. These tangible resources will also help the organization generate revenues. When these resources become old, they will not be able to deliver great returns. Many times employees complain about faulty machines that often malfunction. Sometimes the machinery even malfunctions in front of the customer, which is an embarrassment to the organization and employee.

But even though some organizations have the money to invest in new machinery, they continue to keep some old machines because they do not want to make that financial investment. This approach may actually be costlier as faulty equipment can cause some tasks to be repeated, which is a duplication of effort. The organization may also lose its customers and employees and get several product returns.

8.5 Settling liabilities and payables

When an organization is able to recover, it should acknowledge those who helped it when it was on its knees. They must be adequately repaid in a timely manner.

There are some organizations that recovered but suddenly forgot those that helped them. Your organization should not be among them because you are expected to repay those who helped you. An organization should not turn its back on those who helped it.

Many organizations have liabilities. Not only small and financially challenged organizations have liabilities. Some organizations use liabilities and payables to help propel their organizations.

If liabilities and payables are managed properly, then an organization may have an added opportunity to build more muscles. Some organizations are willing to provide credit to others whose reputation is within the accepted credit limits. This might have happened because of previous healthy relationships and the ability to repay within a reasonable time frame. Many organizations have gone through financial challenges, but once they recover, they should settle outstanding debts.

8.6 Establishing outlets (branches)

Once an organization regains its strength, it is time to extend your reach to different places. This includes, but is not limited to, the establishment of branches, stores, outlets, etc. Many organizations that have established outlets are able to benefit from the additional revenues and manage their risks today.

Some branches can be extremely profitable. All organizations need some cash cow. These can be outlets or strategic business units (SBUs) that will constantly generate much cash (ACCA P5, 2010). Every organization needs much cash on a regular basis, and the outlet may provide that opportunity.

It is important to make sure that the SBUs are adequately staffed and have the quantity or resources needed to meet the needs of the customers. They should be able to operate almost like the parent company. Some of these SBUs, once properly located, can help an organization to have constant success and increase its customer base. It might be important to maintain the same prices for items at the SBU, but in some cases, there may be a price differential, where additional charges may apply to some items.

Organizations which have failed to establish outlets may have died quickly because of challenging moments. They may not have supported outlets and had to stand up to all the pressures. Now that the organization has recovered, then it is time to establish a new strategy and expand its operations.

The cost of raw materials and transport might be lower in certain county/province. This benefit may be maximized with the use of outlets.

A striving organization ought to duplicate itself in many different locations. The establishment of outlets will allow an organization to manage some of its risks.

9. Sharing Your Experience of Recovery with Others

Not everyone who was provided with medical attention when they were dying survived. However, since you survived, then it is important to teach others about the lessons you have learned. These lessons might be able to save many persons and organizations.

9.1 Documenting your views and definition of success

Many persons sometimes fall into the pit they have previously fallen into. Your success should provide you with an opportunity to look back at your past. Once you see the areas which have caused you many problems, then it is important to document them.

Organizations that are involved in risk management should establish a risk register so that they can document the risk that they faced, and the action taken (ACCP P1, 2009). Some persons in the organization do not think that they have to record what happened. That may be their belief, but sometimes you can learn from your own mistakes.

No one may be able to remember everything, but when it is recorded, many persons will be able to benefit from the lessons. Learning from your past may provide an opportunity to become better at what is placed before you.

Those who learn from their past, or the past of another, may be able to achieve significant success in the future. Documenting past bad experiences may be time-consuming and painful, but it will definitely provide a good gauge, which may prevent you from repeating the same bad experience.

With family businesses, when bad experiences are recorded and appropriate actions are taken, other family members will be able to learn from the previous generation. With corporations and other multi-organizations, recording past challenges can help those who will be entrusted with the opportunity to manage the organization. They will have a point of reference to avoid certain pitfalls.

Many persons were able to recover, but not many learned from past mistakes since they did not share their stories. Some organizations have carefully documented their history, and many are able to read it and avoid some of the problems that they may encounter.

9.2 Learning from the past

The past should not be considered as a bad period, especially for organizations which experienced challenges. Many persons who have learned from the past are able to make a great impact for the future. The past provides many learning opportunities. Some past experiences may not be enjoyable to remember. However, if the lesson has been learned from the past and a similar situation occurs in the future, those who are given the opportunity to manage the organization will know what needs to be done.

When faced with certain challenges, sometimes start-up organizations do not know what to do since it might be the first time that they are experiencing such situation. Some organizations have taken an approach to ensure that their senior management team includes some experienced persons. Those experienced persons will be able to provide quality guidance to the younger management team, which can save them from many pitfalls.

Certain experiences are not easy to achieve. However, those who have learned from tough experiences will be able to guide others in the right direction. This is similar to a parent who shares some experiences with his or her child. Children are sometimes of the belief that they have a good grasp of life, but when certain situations confront them, they recognize that they need their parents or that they should have taken their parents' advice.

Past experiences are a good learning tool to avoid future challenges of the same nature from recurring. When an organization is planning for the future, it should also consider some of its past experiences. This will help its assumption and estimates to be all inclusive and not made as though all things will be perfect.

Some organizations will use statistics for future projections. One such statistic is average or mean. This will allow the organization to use a figure that comprises good and bad results. The choice to use this option may have advantages and disadvantages, but something must be used as the basis for future projections.

9.3 Avoiding pitfalls

All people and organizations will experience pitfalls. They are a part of life. However, avoiding pitfalls will be a good thing. Since everyone will face pitfalls in different forms sometime in their lives, then they must be prepared to avoid them.

Organizations must employ persons who are knowledgeable and experienced to be able to see ahead and put measures in place to avoid pitfalls. The strategies to be employed by the organization should be carefully considered, and some "what-if" scenarios must be factored into the strategies since life is not perfect.

As an organization, there are times when potholes are deliberately set in front of your path. Those who can detect potholes may use a different route or reduce their speed and pass through the pothole, while some persons do not exercise much care. However, those who are concerned about the vehicle they are using, especially if it is their personal vehicle, may exercise much caution. If a driver speeds over a pothole, it might cause more harm to the vehicle than expected. Not all aspects of life can be dealt with using speed!

The best efforts of an organization may not be sufficient enough to avoid potholes. However, when potholes are visible, then quick action must be taken by those who have the steering in their hands. When those who oversee the organization panic because of a pothole within their near view, then those who journey with them may also panic.

Leading people has never been an easy task. When you see danger, you have to act normal. This will put those who depend on you at ease. It does not mean that the problem does not exist, but you cannot show signs of discomfort as a leader since your followers may suddenly take a different route, and everyone may meet their own destination without success.

Many organizations may go through trying times, but the leaders in the organization should keep a stable head. Thinking and looking for success is often necessary for all leaders. The organization may never go forward if everyone panics and becomes fainthearted.

9.4 Identifying stumbling blocks

Some stumbling blocks are very common to people. In business, these are easy to be identified. Since the stumbling blocks are easier to be identified, then corrective action must be taken to avoid the known stumbling blocks.

Figure 17. Some identifiable stumbling blocks

Once the management in the organization is able to identify these stumbling blocks, then strategies must be developed for the success of the organization.

When law enforcement officers are planning a major operation, they must consider the opportunities and the challenges that they are likely to face. If they cannot identify the challenges, then they may not be able to accomplish their target.

Once each stumbling block has been identified, the organization should think how it should approach that situation. Some situations can be avoided, but there are others that you will have to confront. Not all situations can be avoided.

10. Improvements

Once the organization has recovered, then it is time to look deep within and find ways to improve. Just like a patient, it might have been discharged from the hospital because it has shown signs of improvement concerning the health issues affecting it. However, being discharged from the medical facility does not mean that you are in perfect health. Some steps need to be taken toward full recovery. The recovery process may be long for some and short for others. The recovery process may be very delicate for some organizations, and for others, they can recover with some external help.

10.1 Collecting the right medication

Before an organization chooses to leave its temporary support stream (saline), it must ensure it is knowledgeable of what is required to be done. Any patient who leaves the hospital or doctor's office without having medication may become sick again if incorrect medication is used.

The organization which has been rescued should work on those areas that were recommended for improvements. Do not try to fix areas which were not affecting you before you were rescued. Keep your eyes focused on those areas which were challenging to you and which caused the organization to have health issues.

To be healthier, the organization must constantly use the medication (solutions) on a regular basis, as was prescribed by your rescuer. Avoid deviating from the recommendations offered as much as possible.

10.2 Checking with your medical officer regularly

While the organization might have used the medication, there may be a need to check with the medical officer who gave you the recommendations for your organization. Some organizations have gotten so big that they avoid checking with those who rescued them. While that might have been the practice for some, it should not be the case with your organization.

As you progress, there may be a need to recommend other things that might be essential. Some of the new recommendations may allow your organization to progress faster. Future recommendations from the rescuer may help you gain additional strength and ability to withstand similar attacks on your organization.

As you check with those who provided you with recommendations, they might be able to share with you any advance information that will help your organization to be resilient. Recovery is not an overnight thing, but a work in progress. Because it is a work in progress, steady reviews are essential for full recovery, and the organization should be engaged in regular reviews.

10.3 Continuous improvement

An organization may have successes, which may only require small changes in the organization. These successes may be greater than the level of change the organization has implemented. Many organizations are happy to make a small improvement but receive success which is greater and allows the organization to recover and be joyful.

Improvement means to make something better (Slack, 2014). All operations, no matter how well-managed, are capable of improvement (Slack, 2014).

Continuous improvement is a deliberate effort by an individual or an organization to increase its efficiencies in an incremental manner (Slack et al., 2015). Continuous improvement methods like Total Quality Management and Six Sigma stress incremental progress, striving for inch-by-inch gains again and again in a never-ending stream (Thompson et al., 2014).

No organization must feel that they are so safe that they do not need to improve. When an organization fails to improve, it may return to a state where sickness may engulf the life of the organization.

There should be a deliberate and constant effort to look for areas of improvement. All staff within the organization should be willing to share their views of how the organization can improve. The senior officers should also be willing to allow employees to share relevant views. Often, some senior officers are of the view that the junior employees cannot share any relevant view. That is not true as the junior employees may have many of the answers needed for the success of the organization.

Figure 18. Deciding whether to incur cost for improvement

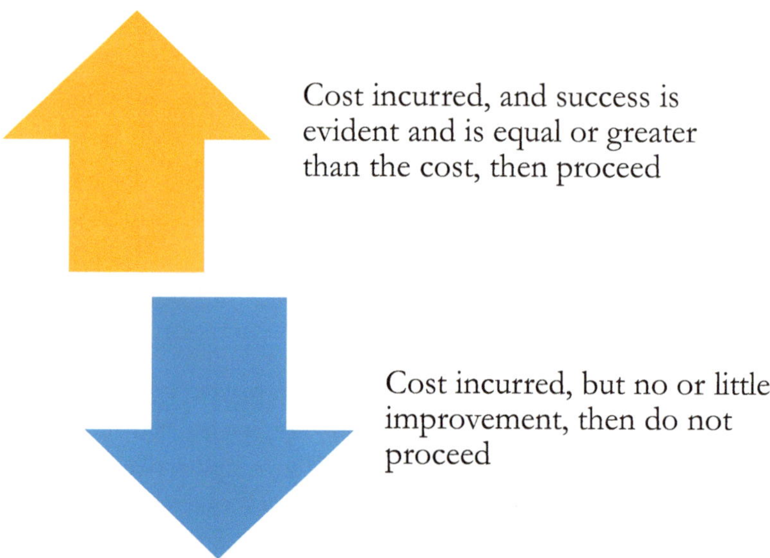

10.4 Business process reengineering and redesigning

The use of cross-functional teams has been popularized by the practice of business process reengineering, which involves radically redesigning and streamlining the workflow (often enabled by cutting-edge use of online technology and information systems), with the goal of achieving quantum gains in performance of the activity (Thompson et al., 2014).

Quality management has developed from an inspection-based process to a philosophy of business that emphasizes customer satisfaction, the elimination of waste and the acceptance of responsibility for conformance with quality specifications at all stages of all business processes (ACCA P5, 2010).

The quick recovery of the organization will require a different approach. Some organizations that require radical success may venture into business process reengineering.

Approaches for recovery should not be long-winded, but quick and suitable. Some organizations may need a sudden injection of finance to help with its recovery. This may be through the form of loans and other forms of financing.

There are also times where the organization may have to replace some of its Human Capital. This may then require the organization to employ specialized persons, whose input will allow the organization to gain quick and consistent success.

The need to replace some machinery, equipment and tools may all aid in the quick success of the organization. When tools and machinery are old, their performance may not be the same as when they were initially acquired. Some of the failures of organizations were as a result of maintaining old and damaged equipment and machinery.

Organizations that make investments to replace items that are essential for their growth may soon reap the benefits of their investments. Organizations must not see the investment as incurring additional cost alone, but incurring it in a strategic manner with the intention of receiving benefits.

11. Planning for Future Success

Any organization that wants success cannot live for today only but should plan for tomorrow as well!

It is a known fact "that tomorrow is not promised to anyone". However, many opportunities may become available, and those organizations that have carefully planned for tomorrow might be able to reap these opportunities.

11.1 Competitions

In business, there will be competition. Some of the competition will not go away and will remain persistent, so the organization must find ways of surviving.

When organizations commenced business, they were probably the only one in operation. But suddenly, many other organizations followed a similar pattern. This is because success attracts more organizations to follow. If your organization is growing fast, then other organizations may want to experience a success like yours or even a better performance. If an organization is able to offer a monopoly product or service, then it may have some easy, but such easy may be indefinite since someone would want to be a part of such success and may do everything possible to break that monopoly.

Competition is an age-old problem, and sometimes, "only the fittest will survive". The success of an organization should not be because of the absence of competition. Many organizations will be extremely happy if there is no competition, but the customer benefits from it.

Those organizations that are offering unfair competition will soon recognize that they may have to follow the correct course of action when competition surrounds them. Customers will now be in a position to save money as prices will be reduced and quality will be enhanced because of competition.

With competition, organizations have to keep thinking of better ways to deliver the same product or service. They cannot be complacent. Some customers rejoice when competition becomes available as they will have more funds to keep in their pockets.

11.2 Opportunities

Opportunities are always there; however, not everyone will see them. Only those capable of seeing and understanding how to connect with them will be able to gain success.

An organization should encourage its human capital to plan for the future. The senior officers should continue to deliberately look for opportunities. Some opportunities are not easily seen, but those who have a careful eye and a probing mind might be able to see them.

Through opportunities, a dying organization may be able to fully recover and help many other organizations. When organizations are under pressure, they may see that an opportunity exists. While the timing may be good, it is not right to wait for problems to exist before identifying opportunities.

An organization should constantly have its employees look for opportunities to grow and find new grounds. It may grow past its normal space and need a new space to operate in. A new space may bring new challenges, as well as opportunities that can change the fortune of the organization.

Several organizations do not allow their junior employees to feed them with opportunities. The senior officers think that they are the only ones who can see and think of opportunities. That is a myth. Junior and ordinary employees can also see opportunities. Those who have a responsibility to guide the organization should be able to incorporate the views of all employees.

When junior employees are given the opportunity to share their ideas and participate in the development of the organization, they get extremely excited and keep thinking of new opportunities. They are often at the last end of the organization structure and they may know of opportunities that many senior employees do not know of. Whenever customers have complaints, most of the time, they share their views with the employees with whom they come into contact. Many customers will take out their frustration on the junior employees.

Many times, opportunities do not wait at a particular place for persons. But the person may need to visit places, and during those times, they may see some opportunities. This is similar to the relationship between a man and a woman. Their relationship might have started because of a location that either of them went to, without the intention of establishing a relationship, but suddenly, they make contact with each other, and then the relationship begins.

Those persons responsible for guiding the organization should be willing to go places and look for opportunity. If they continue to be at the same place, then they may get the same results, and the organization may soon die because of lack of new ideas.

11.3 Risk appetite

Risk is a condition in which there exists a quantifiable dispersion in the possible outcomes from any activity (ACCA P1, 2009).

When opportunities become available, those who will lead the organization should have the willingness to go for the challenge. Every challenge has its risk, but there may be an equal or greater reward. The reward may not be known from the beginning, but during the process.

Figure 19. Risk occurs between opportunities and rewards

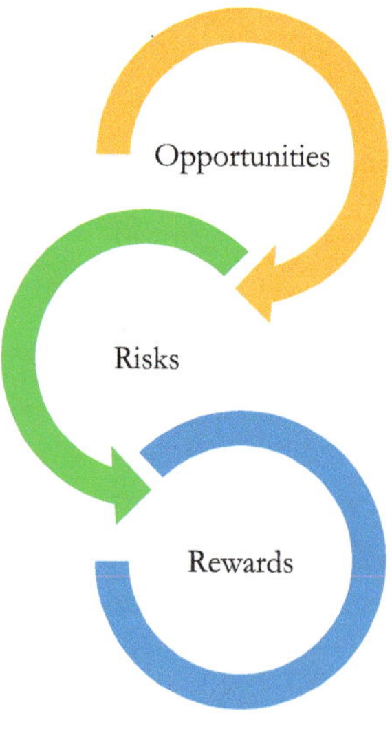

There are often opportunities available, but some persons will not venture out to maximize these opportunities. It must be known that the rewards do not become available until the decision is made to maximize the opportunities. Between the opportunity and the reward is the risk. Its magnitude may not be known at the beginning, and sometimes the risk will surprise the best of planners. For example, someone wants to renovate their building. They hire a contractor to provide them with an estimate of what it will cost them to repair a leaking roof. The contractor provides an estimate. When the contractor begins to repair the leaking roof, they discover that some other items need replacing. This increases the time, cost and scope of the work.

On the other hand, another situation may be that the leaking roof does not need the level of attention proposed. However, the risk may only be known before the process begins.

The success of an organization, as it relates to the opportunities that exist, may only be known when the task is taken, but those who lead the organization should be willing to take some amount of risk.

Some organizations that have embraced corporate governance have established a board of directors, which includes various committees. One such committee is the risk committee, as shown below.

Figure 20. Board committees of an organization

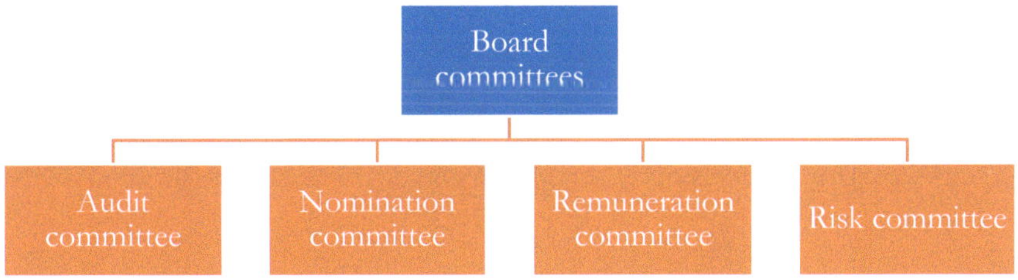

(Extracted from ACCA P1, 2009)

Each committee has its own function. Therefore, the persons selected for the committee must have their own skill set and technical knowledge to help the committee. Those on the risk committee should be willing to take some amount of risk. Sometimes, the failure of the organization is caused by the risk committee not wanting to take risks.

There are also situations where persons on the risk committee want to take too many risks. They are willing to consume any opportunity that presents itself without adequately assessing the situation.

Table 6. Board committees with their definitions

Type of committee	Explanation
Internal audit committee	Arguably the most important committee responsible for liaising with external audit, supervising internal audit and reviewing the annual accounts and internal controls
Nomination committee	Responsible for recommending the appointments of new directors to the board
Remuneration committee	Responsible for advising on the executive director remuneration policy and the specific package for each director
Risk committee	Responsible for overseeing the organization's risk response and management strategies

(Extracted from ACCA P1, 2009)

Below are the risk preferences which will become available to anyone. These preferences may not become available at all once and will vary based on situations.

Table 7. Risk preference

Risk Preference	Explanation
Risk averse	A decision maker who acts on the assumption that the worst outcome might occur

Risk neutral	A decision maker who is concerned with what will be the most likely outcome
Risk seeker	A decision maker who is interested in the best outcome no matter how small the chance that they may occur

(Extracted from ACCA P5, 2010)

When an organization wants to utilize an opportunity, it must consider the possible action to be taken if a particular risk occurs. Risks will occur, but how the management responds to it is very important. As they say, you do not need to take a hammer to hurt an ant, yet you do not need to use a piece of paper to harm an elephant. Appropriate action should be taken to address certain situations.

Figure 21. Possible actions to be taken for risks

(Extracted from ACCA P1, 2009)

The diagram below provides some insights into those organizations desirous of taking risks and compares them with those that choose not to take risks. Remember that many rewards are available for those that take risks.

Figure 22. Organizations that take risk and those that remain constant will face challenges

12. Visionary Captain (Leader)

Opportunities may not make themselves available to those sleeping, but those who have their eyes opened and are looking for opportunities may find them. Still, not everyone who has their eyes open may see the opportunities!

Have a visionary captain is necessary. A visionary captain often scopes the environment, looking for opportunities and areas of improvement. They may look through a small binocular and see very far, while others may look through larger objects but see small things.

Figure 23. A binocular

Extracted from <u>http://www.bigoptics.c, Kunming Binger Co. Ltd)</u>

The visionary captain who has to look through the binocular cannot always depend on everyone to tell him or her what they saw. Each visionary captain should see for himself or herself. Therefore, he or she should be very observant.

12.1 Be proactive, see the future for yourself

When an organization is having challenges, the visionary captain will have to seek ways of rescuing the organization. Some persons may be happy for the demise of the organization. However, a visionary captain should understand that many organizations go through a very lonely path in life, but once a pulse is found in the organization, then it may be time to recover.

You have to open your eyes and mind for what is in store. Do not shut yourself away.

The future is filled with opportunities, but the visionary captain should be able to capitalize on the visions available. Every organization that had a vision for one year will need to review their vision. Time is changing, events are changing, people are changing, so the organization is also expected to change.

Each visionary captain should see for themselves. If the captain leaves that important task to another person, the organization may head into a direction where the leader is not willing to support.

When a boat is sailing, the captain is expected to ensure that the boat goes to the correct destination. In the event that the boat encounters challenges along the way, the captain should make a wise decision in taking the boat to a safe and secure location. Many persons on the boat may be relaxing, sleeping, or doing a task that they think is important, but it is the captain's job to take the boat to the correct destination.

Figure 24. Common places and events where vision may be gained

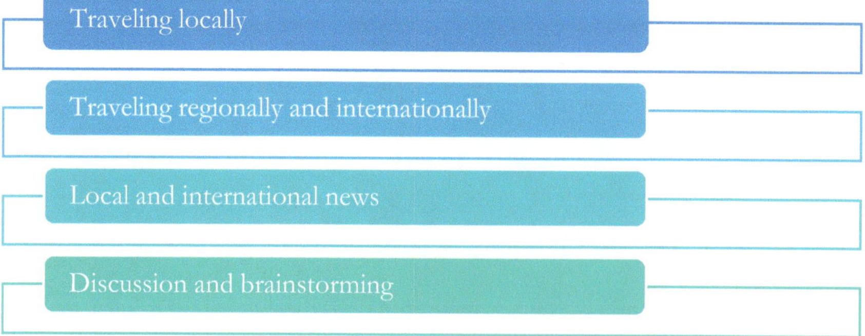

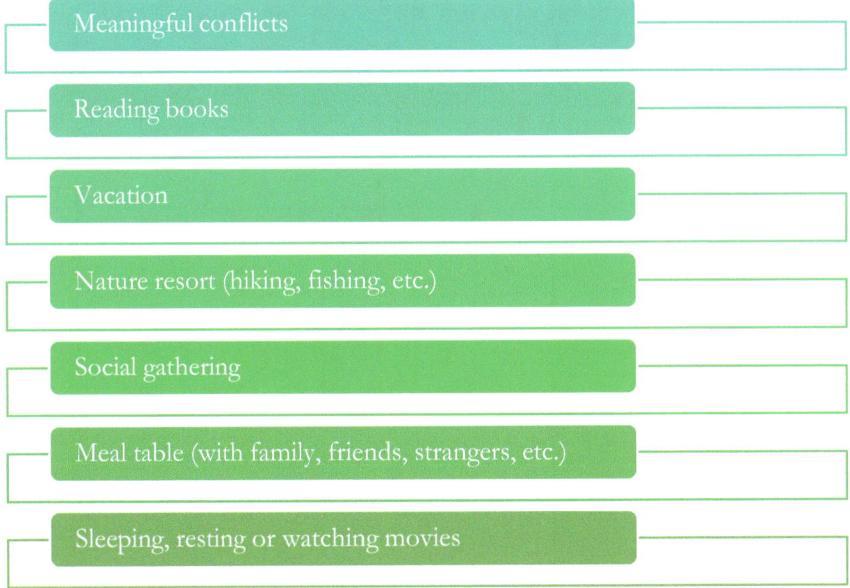

A visionary captain cannot shut away him or herself from life and expect to gain vision always. There are times when shutting away oneself may be important, but that should not be the norm. Some visionary captains receive new vision while taking a child to school, shopping, relaxing, etc. With more exposures, a visionary captain may have a fresh inspiration.

12.2 Document your vision, enact your environment

Visionary captains can become so excited with the vision that they want to implement it immediately or celebrate. However, the brain can retain many things, and it may not always remember everything. Therefore, recording the vision is important. Not all the vision may be given to you in a sequential manner, but when the vision is recorded, you might be able to put some clothes on the skeleton.

A documented vision may provide great strength to a visionary captain when they are tired and run out of ideas. When a visionary captain is confronted with the many challenges of life, a vision may provide them impetus that the captain needs to take the boat to its intended location.

Do not discard your vision, but check it very often so that you remain on course and able to fulfill that vision. The vision should not be forgotten but should be close enough for the leader to have hope for the future. The vision often helps the organization to remain focused and stick to one direction. Once the leader is able to channel the energy of the people of that organization in one direction, then great success is expected throughout the organization, which should be the ultimate goal.

A documented vision should become available not only to the captain but also to all players within the organization. Often, it is said that the followers do not know the direction the organization is heading since the leader has not disclosed it to the other employees.

When employees are aware of the vision, they may coordinate their knowledge and skills to help the future of the organization. If more hands are to do the same thing, then less time will be spent on dealing with conflicts.

12.3 Tell selected people about your vision

Informing people of your vision is good, but not everyone must be informed. They are some persons who may not appreciate you and disapprove of your vision. Never share your vision with your competitor. When competitors know your vision, they may want to engage in activities that may derail you.

Knowing that not everyone will support your vision, then selecting the persons to whom you will share the vision with is important. The success of an organization is not a "one-man army". When other persons know the vision and support it, then they may provide additional guidance that will help with its implementation. Having the vision is only one task. Executing the vision is essential for the success of the organization.

Figure 25. The implementation of the vision is better

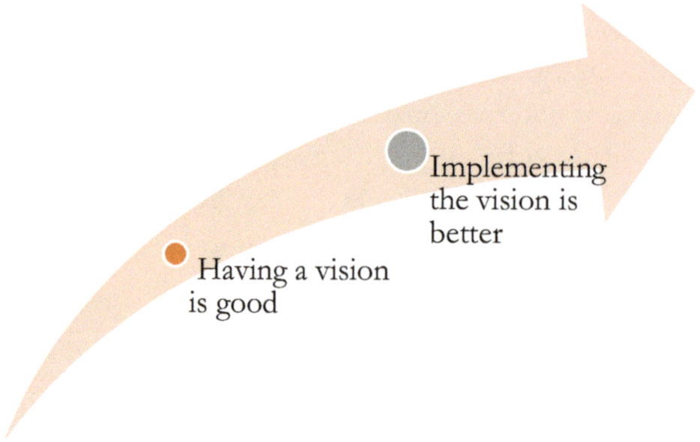

Some persons are so happy to help you bring your vision into reality. You must look for such persons and connected with them. If they are going to help you with the success of your vision, then you must be open with them to share relevant information. They may, in turn, share some essential ideas with you which will help fast-track your vision.

You may not always have the finances for the vision you have, but by sharing the vision with selected and trusted persons, they might be able to help finance your vision or direct you to some source of financing. Some visions may be bigger than your financial resource can afford.

As you share your vision, you should also expect to answer some questions and receive constructive criticism. If you do not want constructive criticism, then you may only have "yes men" around you. They may see some areas in the vision that needs additional support, but they will not tell you of any shortcomings. If you surround yourself with "yes people," it might only be a matter of time before you and the vision fail. The vision is too important to fail! So take as much advice as possible from reliable and honest persons so that you can help the organization succeed. The success of your vision can impact the lives of many persons and the nation as a whole. Therefore, make your vision a reality.

12.4 Passionately working with your vision

It is not practical for persons to run with your vision. You must be there to work your vision through to fruition. Many persons might have provided great advice and support, but the success of the vision often depends on the amount of effort and energies you put into it.

When an organization elects persons to be part of the board of directors, they should work toward the same vision and not take a different route. Everyone must pool their efforts and constantly work with the same vision.

The person who received the vision should play a part in its execution. If the supporting members recognize that the visionary captain is least interested, then they may take a similar approach, which may lead to the death of the organization.

Some organizations die because the visionary captain has decided not to be involved in the implementation of the vision. When the vision is at its initial stage, much effort should be exercised to make it a reality. Members cannot take a relaxing position.

The visionary captain should find a group of people who are willing and able and have some amount of knowledge to assist with the implementation of the vision of the organization. There are times when the leaders may do all the work necessary in implementing the vision. However, some visions are huge, and the help of many persons will be needed. The earlier these persons can be assembled and given clear directions, the faster the organization will succeed.

There will be some amount of challenges with persons in the group. That is a regular feature with most groups. They will go through these stages, but their focus should be to implement the vision.

Table 8. Group development stages

Forming	It is characterized by the gathering of superficial information about fellow members and low trust.
Storming	It is usually marked by intragroup conflict, heightened emotional levels and status differentiation as remaining contenders struggle to build alliances and fulfill the group's leadership role.
Norming	The clear emergence of a leader and development of group norms and cohesiveness are the key indicators of this stage of group development.
Performing	Group members play functional, interdependent roles that are focused on the performance of the group tasks.

(Extracted from Hughes et al., 2016, p. 397)

While there are hurdles in the path of the group and the visionary captain, everyone should keep calm and work toward delivering the desired results. At the early stage of the group, there may be many conflicts, and some members may be derailed from the vision. The visionary captain should bring all members of the group into conformity. If the visionary captain takes a hands-off approach, then the vision may die.

The more the visionary leader presses toward the vision, those who might have not believed in the vision may soon join and support the effort for the success of the organization.

13. Connecting with the Public (Marketing)

An organization which has been rescued and has fully recovered should be connected with the public. Many organizations experience financial difficulty, and one of the reasons is that they fail to connect with the public.

As time progresses, competition increases. Therefore, those organizations that fail to keep the public connected may lose their customers. Once your organization begins to lose its important customers, then that will cause a financial challenge for your organization.

No organization that wants to enter the market will seek your permission, but they will enter and engage customers. Some of the customers they will connect with will be those persons that you have. Therefore, there will be a constant fight for the same customers, and your organization should not give into that fight but put up a strong resistance.

13.1 Competition

Organizations will continue to face competition. If your organization is selling certain products, competition is likely to occur. If your organization is buying a particular product, then it will also have its own set of challenges. Porter's Five Forces model provides some important information about the force that many organizations will face. Organizations are not free from challenges.

Figure 26. Porter's Five Forces Model

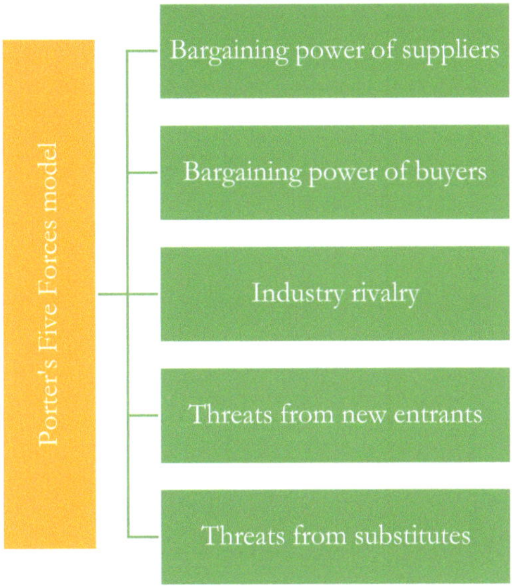

(Extracted from Thompson et al., 2014)

Despite an organization's best attempt to stay away from competition, that desire may not become a reality.

Many organizations die because of the forces which were applied to them and them not being able to resist those challenges. While that might have happened to some organizations, that should not be your position. Your organization should not be counted among those that started and died.

Therefore, your organization must fight daily to be in business. Your organization must be ethical in all that it does and keep the customers informed.

Table 9. Pressure from competition

Types of competition
Competitive pressures created by rivalry among competing sellers
• Rivalry increases when buyer demand is growing slowly or declining.

Rapidly expanding buyer demand produces enough new business for all industry members to grow without using volume-boosting sales tactics to draw customers away from rival enterprises.

- Rivalry increases as it becomes less costly for buyers to switch brands. The less costly it is for buyers to switch their purchases from one seller to another, the easier it is for sellers to steal customers away from rivals.
- Rivalry increases as the products of rival sellers become less strongly differentiated. When the offerings of rivals are identical or weakly differentiated, buyers have less reason to be brand loyal, a condition that makes it easier for rivals to convince buyers to switch to their offerings.
- Rivalry is more intense when there is excess supply or unused production capacity, especially if the industry's product has high fixed costs or high storage costs.
- Rivalry intensifies as the number of competitors increases and they become more equal in size and capacity.
- Rivalry becomes more intense as the diversity of competitors increases in terms of long-term directions, objectives, strategies and countries of origin.
- Rivalry is stronger when high exit barriers keep unprofitable firms from leaving the industry.

Competitive pressures associated with the threats of new entrants

- Cost advantages enjoyed by industry incumbents
- Strong brand preferences and high degrees of customer loyalty
- Strong "network effects" in customer demand
- High capital requirements
- The difficulties of building a network of distributions or dealers and securing adequate space on retailer's shelves
- Restrictive government policies

Competitive pressures from the sellers of substitute products

- Whether substitutes are readily available and attractively priced
- Whether buyers view the substitutes as being comparable or better in

terms of quality, performance and other relevant attributes
* Whether the costs that buyers incur in switching to the substitutes are low or high

Competitive pressures stemming from suppliers' bargaining power

* When demand from suppliers' products are high and they are in short supply
* Whether suppliers provide a different input that enhances the performance of the industry's product
* Whether it is difficult or costly for industry members to switch their purchases from one supplier to another
* Whether the supplier industry is dominated by a few large companies and whether it is more concentrated than the industry it sells to
* Whether suppliers provide an item that accounts for a sizable fraction of the costs of the industry's products
* Whether it makes good economic sense for industry members to integrate backward and self-manufacture items they have been buying from suppliers
* Whether there are good substitutes available for the suppliers' products
* Whether industry members are major customers of suppliers

Competition from buyers' bargaining power and price sensitivity

* Buyer power increases when buyer demand is weak in relation to industry supply.
* Buyer power increases when industry goods are standardized or differentiation is weak.
* Buyers' bargaining power is greater when their costs of switching to competing brands or substitutes are relatively low.
* Buyers have more power when they are large and few in numbers relative to the number of sellers.
* Buyers gain leverage if they are well-informed about sellers' products, prices and costs.

- Buyers' bargaining power is greater when they pose a credible threat of integrating backward into the business of sellers.
- Buyer leverage increases if buyers have discretion to delay their purchases or perhaps even not make a purchase at all.
- Buyer price sensitivity increases when buyers are earning low profits or have low income.

(Extracted from Thompson et al., 2014, pp. 50–63)

Competition will always be there, faced by almost any organization. For some, they have to constantly find strategies to be competitive, while others have an easier time doing business since they have little to no competition. An organization that wants to be successful must be willing to apply enough pressure to fight off competition. Some organizations that want to remain competitive find solutions, such as gaining significant market shares and becoming market leaders.

Figure 27. Competition can aid growth or death

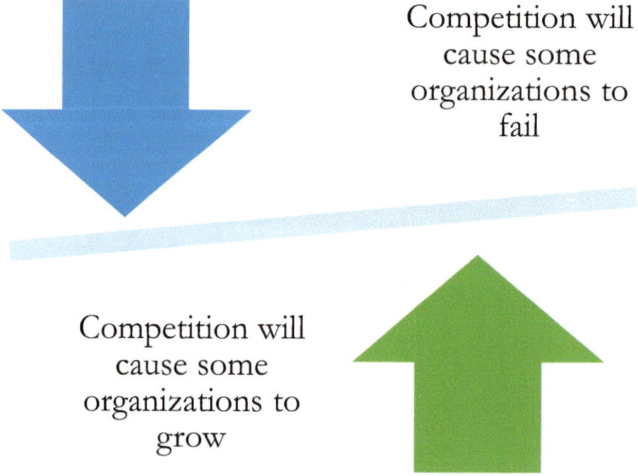

Even if an organization has been in existence for decades, it may still experience some competition. Those organizations that have faced several competitions over the years might have built muscles to deal with them to prevail. But those that are new to the market may find it difficult to stay alive. Many new organizations may quickly exit the market because of strong competition. However, those that survived and continue to face competition probably used some of these weapons to remain in business.

Table 10. Common "weapons" for competing with rivals

Type of competitive weapon
Offering price discounts and clearance sales
Couponing and advertising items on sale
Advertising product or service characteristics and using ads to enhance a company's image
Innovating to improve product performance and quality
Introducing new or improved features and providing a greater product selection
Increasing customization of a product or service
Building a bigger, better dealer network
Improving warranties and offering low-interest financing

(Extracted from Thompson et al., 2014, p. 53)

13.2 Public relation and advertising

Public relations involve a variety of programs directed internally to employees of the company or externally to consumers, other firms, the government, and the media to promote or protect a company's image or its individual products (Kotler et al., 2013).

Some organizations that died might have been a result of them not keeping the public informed that they are in business and that they have something to offer to the public. It is surprising to know that some organizations are very timid in informing the public that they have what they need.

There are so many ways to engage the public, yet some organizations have not utilized them, which is why it is no surprise that some hidden organizations have already died. Organizations should no longer hide in a closet and expect persons to know that they are in existence.

Advertising is any paid form of nonpersonal presentation and promotion of ideas, goods, or services by an identified sponsor via print, broadcast, network, electronic, and display media (Kotler et al., 2013).

An organization must be willing to spend some money on advertising. A person will not know overnight that your organization is in operation.

Advertising and promotion are important parts of the marketing program of firms that compete in the global marketplace (Belch & Belch, 2015).

Figure 28. Importance of keeping the public informed

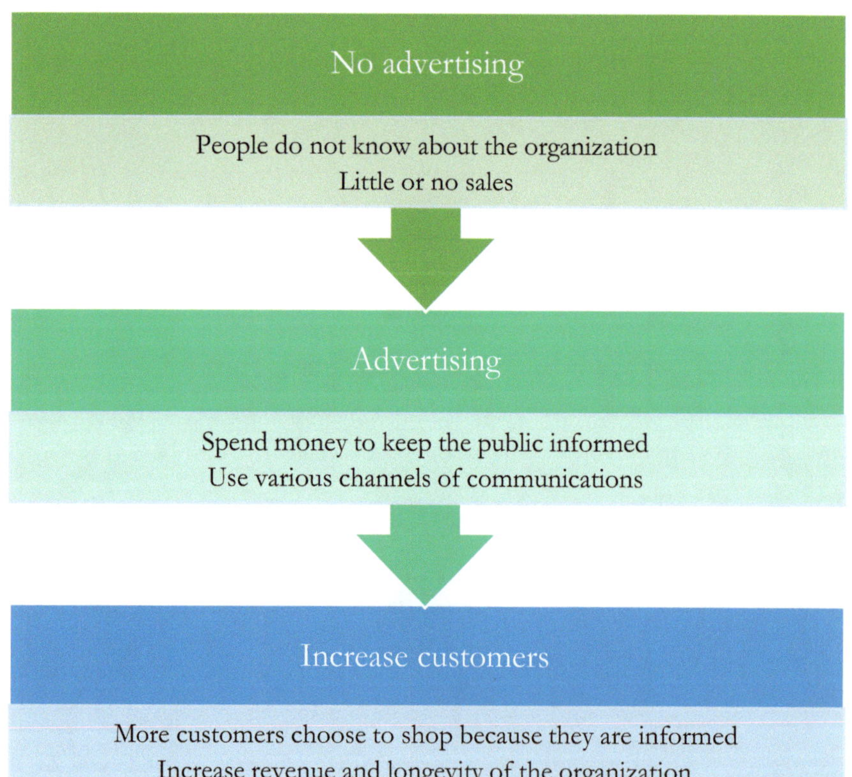

13.3 Marketing research and survey

Marketing research is the systematic design, collection, analysis and reporting of data and findings relevant to a specific marketing situation facing the company (Kotler et al., 2013). The data collection phase of marketing research is generally the most expensive and most prone to error (Kotler et al., 2013).

Organizations that want success and increased revenues must be willing to engage in some amount of research. Many organizations that engage in research are often able to identify the needs of the market and know how to position their products in the market. If an organization operates in ignorance, then it may soon be isolated and die.

There is power in knowledge. To know is a good thing. Those who know must move beyond that stage and make a decision. Once that decision is made, then there must be action. Too often, people know what has to be done but do nothing. Life will not change for those who sit on the knowledge they have.

Below is a marketing research process that many organizations use. It is clear that an organization needs to take some action. Those organizations that fail to take appropriate action contribute to their own failure.

Figure 29. Marketing research process

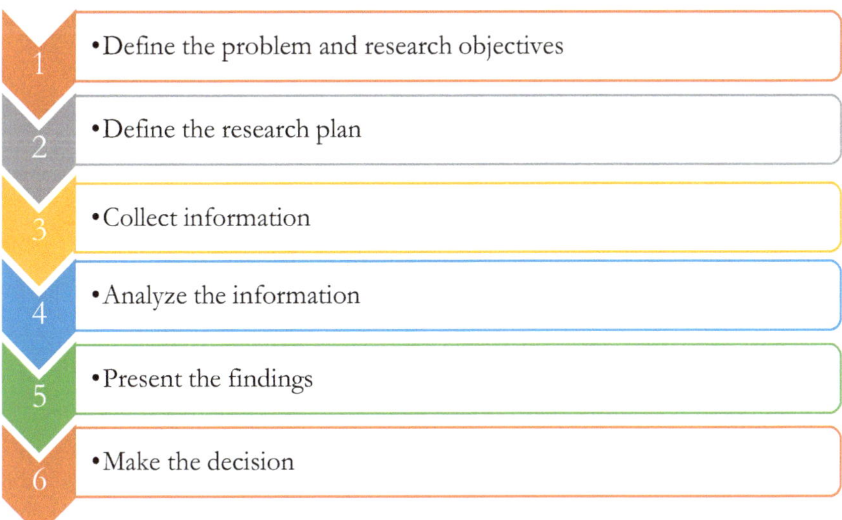

(Extracted from Kotler et al., 2013)

At the end of the research, the management of the organization must understand the information presented and make a careful decision. Sometimes, debating the findings take time debating the findings, but the management must be courageous enough to make a decision. The success of an organization is not how much time is spent thinking, but the quality of the decision that they make.

Figure 30. Survival is more than knowing, but acting

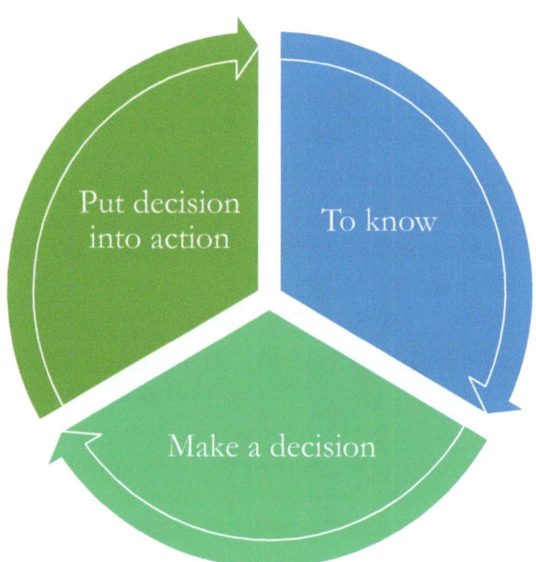

When surveys are carried out, those that manage the organization will have data that they can work with. Those who request the data must determine what is needed and when it is needed.

Once the data is captured, someone must be willing to interpret the data. When templates and other reporting formats are available, then the data can help the organization get information. That information will help the officers of the organization to make a decision.

Some organizations are good at making decisions, but they fail to act on the decision. Any decision without action will result in the death of the organization, and the organization may need a rescue operation.

Any decision and action must be made in a timely manner. An organization that wants to be the leader in the market must be able to make quick decisions and act on those decisions. The market is not sympathetic with those that make decisions but fail to act.

13.4 Marketing

An organization might have been the first mover in the industry, but in modern days, many other organizations may be fast followers (Hill & Hult, 2016).

Marketing is the science and art of delivering a product, service, idea and experience to its intended consumer at an affordable price, thus allowing the organization to maintain profitability (Kotler et al., 2013).

Earlier in this chapter, you read about competition. When there is greater competition, the organization should market its product or service. The plan of competitors is to keep you out of the market, so you must aim to keep them out as well. The cost of marketing may be high, but the organization must decide how much it wants to spend on marketing.

Also, there may be times when the organization has to change the market in which it operates. If the current market becomes saturated, then there may be a need to look for other avenues to keep the public informed of your products. Your product may be the best for customers, but you still have to engage the public. When the public is well-informed about your products and supports them, then you know that you are making an impact. You must not become complacent but should constantly look for ways of improving your products and keeping the public informed.

13.5 Summative and continuous assessment of the organizational performance and new market

When organizations plan, they must be willing to see if their plan is making an impact. Oftentimes, organizations use gap analysis to review its current performance and plan for the future (ACCA P5, 2010).

Every organization should assess both the product and the market. Even though an organization thinks that it has the best plan, the reaction of the public may be different. It cannot keep itself away from the public. It should always try to reach out to them.

The Ansoff Growth Matrix can help an organization assess its performance and find new ways to operate.

Table 11. Ansoff Growth Matrix

Options	Explanation
Market penetration	Current products, current markets
Market development	Current products, new markets
Product development	New products, current markets
Diversification	New products, new markets

(Extracted from ACCA, P5, 2010)

If an organization has exhausted all its options with an existing product and the same market, then there may be a need to look for a new market and a new product. This approach will lead toward diversification. New strategies (e.g., market penetration, market development, product development, diversification and withdrawal) are developed to fill the gap (ACCA, P5, 2010).

Figure 31. Diversification path

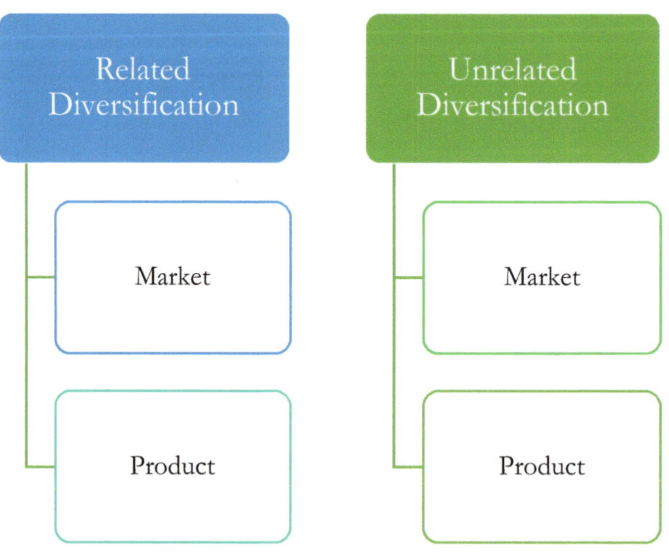

(Extracted from Thompson et al., 2014)

A related diversification strategy involves building the company around a business that has a strategic fit with respect to key value chain activities and competitive assets (Thompson et al., 2014).

Meanwhile, unrelated diversification happens when an organization gets involved in a business or an area of business in which it has no experience or resources (Thompson et al., 2014).

Whether an organization wants to close its gap or not, it must be willing to take swift action to stay alive. And whether it chooses a related or unrelated diversification path, it cannot lose sight of what it wants to do. It will continue to face competition, so it should provide the public with enough information. The public may become a customer based on the information provided by the organization. Some customers find it easy to choose an organization, but others may have to hear the same message repeatedly making a decision.

An organization should not get tired of keeping the public informed of its product and services.

Reference List

1. *A Guide to the Project Management Book of Knowledge (PMBOK)*. 2008. 4th edn. Pennsylvania: Project Management Institute.

2. ACCA. CAT Interactive B2. 1997. *Cost Accounting Systems*. London: BPP Publishing.

3. ACCA P1. 2009. *Professional Accountant*. London: BPP House.

4. ACCA P5. 2010. *Advance Performance Management*. London: BPP House.

5. Belch, G. E. & Belch, M. A. 2015. *Advertising and Promotion: An Integrated Marketing Communications Perspective*. 10th edn. New York: McGraw-Hill.

6. Hill, C. W. L. & Hult, G. T. M. 2016. *Global Business Today*. 9th edn. New York: McGraw-Hill.

7. Hughes, R., Ginnett, R. & Curphy, G. 2015. *Leadership: Enhancing the Lessons of Experience*. 8th edn. New York: McGraw-Hill.

8. Kotler, P., Keller, K. L., Ang, S. H., Leong, S. M. & Tan, C. T. 2013. *Marketing Management: An Asian Perspective*. 6th edn. Singapore: Pearson Education South Asia Pte Ltd.

9. Kotler, P., Keller, K. L., Ang, S. H., Leong, S. M. & Tan, C. T. 2013. *Marketing Management: An Asian perspective*. 6th edn. Singapore: Pearson Education South Asia Pte Ltd.

10. Shields, J., Brown, M., Kaine, S., Dolle-Samuel, C., NorthSamardzic, A., McLean, P., Johns, R., O'Leary, P., Plimmer, G. & Robinson, J. 2016. *Managing Employee Performance and Reward: Concepts, Practices, Strategies*. 2nd edn. Port Melbourne: Cambridge University Press.

11. Slack, N., Brandon-Jones, A., Johnston, R. & Betts, A. 2015. *Operations and Process Management*. 4th edn. Harlow: Pearson Education Limited.

12. Thompson, A. A., Peteraf, M. A., Gamble, J. E. & Strickland, A. J. 2014. *Crafting and Executing Strategy: The Quest for Competitive Advantage, Concepts and Cases*. 19th edn. New York: McGraw-Hill.

About the Author

Some persons know why organizations have failed and are willing to talk about those failures, but few are willing to provide advice to help organizations to be rescued. The information that Geary Reid offers in this book will help organizations to have massive changes and to become organizations that meet the needs of people.

When an organization is about to die, that does not mean that the organization is dead, but it does mean that it needs much help. If the right things are done for the organization, then it can have a revival and move from death to life again. When an organization is about to die, it will also need a visionary captain to steer the organization in another direction, who will help it to have sustained success thereafter. Signs of failure will visit every organization, but what stakeholders do with those signs is the important thing, as their actions can cause the organization to fail or succeed.

9 789768 305060